NO THANK YOU,
MR. PRESIDENT

No Thank You, Mr. President

The Black Dilemma

The Lost Priority

NO THANK YOU, MR. PRESIDENT

MR. PRESIDENT

John Herbers

W·W·NORTON & COMPANY·INC
New York

Copyright © 1976 by W. W. Norton & Company, Inc.
First Edition

Library of Congress Cataloging in Publication Data
Herbers, John.
　No thank you, Mr. President.
　Includes index.
　1. Herbers, John. 2. Journalists—United States—
Correspondence, reminiscences, etc. 3. Watergate
Affair, 1972–　　I. Title.
PN4874.H47A34　1976　　070.4'092'4　　75-35879
ISBN 0-393-05570-1

All Rights Reserved
Published simultaneously in Canada
by George J. McLeod Limited, Toronto

Printed in the United States of America
1 2 3 4 5 6 7 8 9

To my colleagues on the
White House beat

*that they may find a way to separate
imagery from substance, the phony from the real*

CONTENTS

108   109
136   137   138 - 139
140   141

ACKNOWLEDGMENTS

I am grateful to the editors of the *New York Times* and to Clifton Daniel, the Washington bureau chief, for giving me the opportunity to cover the White House during a critical period of its history, an assignment that made this book possible. Throughout I was given a remarkable amount of freedom to pursue the stories I thought important and to shape them to my conception of the truth. It was in the course of developing those stories that I acquired the ideas and observations expressed here. I am indebted, too, to the other *Times* correspondents with whom I shared the beat for a time, for their help and support: R. W. Apple, Jr., Philip Shabecoff, Marjorie Hunter, and Richard L. Madden. Presidential scholars granted me interviews that helped me shape my opinion of what the Presidency ought to be. These included James MacGregor Burns, Henry Steele Commager, Thomas E. Cronin, and Theodore J. Lowi. I was encouraged in an unconventional approach to covering the White House by the example set by some of my colleagues, including Adam Clymer of the *Baltimore Sun*, Norman Kempster of the *Washington Star-News*, Lou Cannon of the *Washington Post*, James Deakin of the *St. Louis Post-Dispatch*, and, especially, John Osborne of the *New Republic*.

INTRODUCTION

In American journalism, there is no beat that compares to that of covering the White House. In the history of the American Presidency, there was no period that compared to the last year and one-half of Richard Nixon's term and the first few months of the Ford administration. Never had a President been forced from office and a non-elected Vice-President moved into his place. It was my good fortune to have been assigned by the *New York Times* to the White House during this period. It was a relatively short assignment. Yet more history, drama, excitement, boredom, frustration, and anxiety were packed into the two years, three months, and twelve days that I spent there than into my prior twenty-two years of reporting. This was true even though I had covered such major events as the civil rights and Vietnam peace movements, riots in the cities, national political campaigns, and various major developments in the federal government.

The White House beat is unique partly because on a day-to-day basis it is usually the source of more important national and international news than any other in Washington. But it is unique for other reasons. It is the one center of news where the press, in deference to the high office and because of the esteem most Americans hold for the Presidency, surrenders much of its independence. The White House assignment has been compared to the police beat of the average American city because the reporter spends so much of his time waiting for those in charge to hand out news. That comparison soon breaks down, however. Correspondence from the police station is subjected to the usually tough standards of what constitutes news before it is printed or put on the air. Events at the White House are

judged by a separate standard. A Presidential utterance need
not be new, interesting, or important to make the front page of
the papers, the lead item on the radio news roundups, or a
major segment of the evening television newscasts. It is considered news because it comes from the President. Furthermore,
the White House in various ways is able to shape much of the
reporting so as to cast the President and his assistants in the
most favorable light, whether or not they deserve it. Although
most Presidents have felt abused by the attacks of editorial
writers and columnists, there can be no doubt that the modern
Presidency has the upper hand in conveying to the public the
President's policies, motives, and intentions as he directs the
government and travels the world.

The aborted second term of Richard Nixon and the ascend-
ency of Jerry Ford, the plain man, provided an unexpected
opportunity for some basic changes in White House press coverage. Yet the habits and conditioning of many years die hard.
Despite my irreverent reflections on the institutionalized
White House and press, as recorded here, I never ceased to
believe that the Presidency offers the best hope for creative
national leadership. But it is now not the office envisioned by
the founding fathers. It has been shackled by its overaggrandizement, its bureaucracy, and its insularity. It has been a long
time since Thomas Jefferson was required to stand in line at a
boarding house for his dinner after he had been inaugurated
President.

If the beat and period of history covered in this book were
unique, the experiences of the reporters involved were at least
unusual, as the following pages will reflect. There can be no
pretending that any of us were mere observers of the passing
scene. We were very deeply involved, as summed up by one
brief episode of mid-1973. Nixon had spent one of his long
weekends in Key Biscayne, Fla., at a time when the Watergate
disclosures were breaking in Washington. For three days, the
President and his aides had shut us out, providing neither comment on the charges nor the answers to questions that piled up
on the conduct of national and international affairs. The heat
and humidity made outdoor activity unbearable, and some of us
had spent too much time trying in vain to reach Presidential

assistants, waiting in the press room for nothing to happen or lounging in a sleazy bar on Miami Beach.

After such a weekend, it was vital for the reporters to get a glimpse of the President, to make sure he was still alive and functioning. We were gathered at Homestead Air Force base as close to the Presidential jet as the Secret Service would permit. The helicopters arrived precisely on schedule from Nixon's compound on Key Biscayne. The President got out smiling and waving to a small crowd of Air Force families gathered at the gate. He was followed aboard the plane by a large entourage of aides and agents, all appearing very aloof and unruffled. Bringing up the rear was King Timahoe II, the President's dog. King, as he was called, was a beautiful Irish setter, with a sleek red coat and a proud head, usually erect. Now, perhaps because of the whine of the jet engines, King had his magnificent tail between his legs and his head ducked very low as he crouched across the runway and had to be prodded up the stairs. It was as if the Presidential party, angered and frustrated over the Watergate disclosures, had spent the weekend abusing poor King, who alone dared to show his feelings. Laughter and merriment, more than the occasion warranted, broke out in the press corps. It was a small reward for a miserable, unproductive weekend, but there was the knowledge that the next day, perhaps, there would be a big and challenging story.

That is the way it is on the White House beat, whoever is addressed as Mr. President.

NO THANK YOU, MR. PRESIDENT

1
THE EMPEROR'S COURT

My most vivid memory of Tokyo is that there were eighty-five pools. Not pools for bathing, but press pools in which the scores of reporters and photographers covering President Ford's visit to Japan were divided and dispersed to strategic points to record all color and minutiae that would be assembled into one unselective panorama for the use of all. If the President and Emperor Hirohito were to dine in the Imperial Palace, for example, there would be a pool stationed at the top of the stairs, another at the bottom and a third in the dining room. Writers of history, if they are interested, can learn from a pool report dated November 19, 1974, that "there were banks of yellow and lavender chrysanthemums on the table which was shaped in the form of a gridiron, a long table with several other tables leading to it. The chrysanthemum is the symbolic flower of Japan and the same chrysanthemum design was used in the pattern of the china on which the dinner was served. There were three wine glasses in front of each place setting. The President sat on the Emperor's right and on Ford's left sat the Empress who wore a pale lavender kimono and diamond encrusted combs in her grey hair which was piled up in Japanese style. . . . The menu included consommé, Managatsuo Oau Vin Blanc; mousse de foi gras; filet of beef a la renaissance, salad and ice cream parfaits. The wines served were Mcc Meursault

Charvet 1970; then Chauteau la Faite Rothschild 1964; and Moet et Chandon Dom Perignon Bruit 1964. Ford appeared to be enjoying every minute of elegant eating. . . ."

I am reminded from the report of Pool Number 476, written on November 21 in Kyoto (by that time the number of pools had swollen considerably), that the President, at a tea house on the lawn of Nijo Castle, tried his hand at the koto, a sixteenth-century musical instrument. "Ford tried to get the picks on his fingertips but they wouldn't fit. He finally took one between the thumb and forefinger and managed to strike a few melodious notes while the girls giggled appreciatively."

And so on. But I find very little in my files or my memory on the meaning of the trip. As the Presidential caravan moved across the landscape of Northeast Asia—from Japan to Korea to Vladivostok—I was impressed, as I had been many times, by what a strange and unique institution this was—the Presidency of the United States.

It was almost as if the Queen of England, with no authority to govern, had undertaken an extensive foreign tour in which ceremony was everything. The large press apparatus maintained by the White House was tuned to disclose everything about the ceremony. The President was reported, rather casually by his press officers, to be conducting the business of the United States government along the way. But a reporter's suspicion and instinct were that precious little was done. There was too much time spent in movement, in official greetings, in parades, in sight-seeing. Attention focused on such things as the pants Mr. Ford wore with his morning coat—they were too short, a fact his speech writers and public relations people seized on with glee as grist for Presidential humor in the days to come. Yet the American Presidency was not designed to be a ceremonial office. That was a role that it took on, among many others, as its real powers grew. Through most of the twentieth century the office held so much authority that the President's policies and actions, whatever the character of the occupant of the office, had an impact on the lives of many millions of people around the world. But here was a President acting, with ample precedent, like an idle emperor on a good-will tour.

In Seoul, I received the following cable from Gerald Gold of the *Times'* foreign desk: "Would like you to take a really hard-nosed look at the President's trip after the Japan–Korea visit, as we are struck by the apparent lack of real substance, as you noted in your story today. What is the point of it all? Does it add anything to U. S.–Japan or U. S.–Korean relations? Is Ford just massaging his ego? Is he campaigning? Is Kissinger doing anything out of sight that makes the trip substantive?"

Yes, he was campaigning, for the support and good will of the American people. In recent years, it had been considered essential that the President of the United States be viewed by his constituents as taking the lead in promoting peace and stability around the world, even when he, in fact, was promoting war and intrigue. Ford, a new President who had never been known for his knowledge of foreign affairs, was demonstrating to Americans that he could be an active world leader, just as other Presidents had done. Yet so exalted was the office in the minds of the American electorate that no one in the White House could bring himself to acknowledge that not much more than that was involved. An institution with so much real power does not easily acknowledge that it is engaging more in image-making than in substantive actions. Thus the ambiguity of the Ford trip to Japan and Korea was a classical White House phenomenon, more related to what the office had become in recent years than who happened to be in charge at the moment.

Before I could respond to the cable, the trip moved into a new phase, the talks at Vladivostok between Ford and Soviet leader Leonid I. Brezhnev that resulted in a tentative agreement to place a ceiling on offensive nuclear arms systems. Here was an achievement of substance that was to be measured and debated at length in the months ahead. Yet once again the institution showed another strange aspect of itself, as seen in the behavior of some officials directly under the President.

It was Secretary of State Kissinger who set the tone for this demonstration in the rambling talks he held with reporters aboard the President's plane prior to the Vladivostok meeting. Kissinger always had been his own press agent. Not only did he enjoy talking to reporters, columnists, and editors, but he had an ability to make them like him and convince them he was a man of enormous abilities who was embarked on a sensible course of action, whatever that might be at the moment. He rarely ever made a trip with the President without coming back to the small rear compartment and talking to the pool.

The pool on Air Force One usually consisted of two or three photographers, a reporter for each of the two American wire services, and two or three reporters representing the newspapers, the news magazines, and the broadcasters. As paying passengers aboard the plane—their organizations are assessed their prorata share of first-class fare—they are, nevertheless, given the least desirable quarters. The President and senior members of his party, who board from the front and occupy larger compartments, are free to visit or ignore the reporters as they wish. The reporters are not permitted up front. On trips between Washington and President Nixon's coastal villas the reporters and Air Force personnel aboard shared the compartment with the three Nixon dogs. Dr. Kissinger was the only official aboard in those days who seemed to attach importance to the journalists aboard.

By the time we landed in Vozdvishenka airport near Vladivostok on November 23, there was available—through the various Air Force One pools—a volume of Kissinger statements about the trip under his own name or that of a "senior official," as he liked to be called when he did not wish to be quoted directly. It was the task of the pool to condense, within a limited time, the Kissinger statements for the main body of reporters who traveled aboard separate, commercial planes and thus did not have direct access to the loquacious Dr. Kissinger.

As a member of the Air Force One pool from Seoul to Vladivostok, I recall that we had finished the pool report as the plane was making its landing approach. I was sitting in the aisle pulling on stubborn overshoes for the Siberian snows when once again, for the third time, Kissinger appeared in the rear compartment. While the jet nosed through the clouds for the landing strip, the eminent Secretary of State, standing in shirt sleeves, talked of such ponderous but vital subjects as SALT (Strategic Arms Limitation Talks), European security negotiations, the crisis in the Middle East, and the war in Southeast Asia. Of the Ford–Brezhnev talks, he said, "The Russians didn't come all the way here to have a confrontation. I don't expect a confrontation." This was valuable material in that it signaled a possible breakthrough with the Soviets. But there was no time to write another pool report. An addendum had to be typed aboard a bus on the bumpy road to Vladivostok.

Aside from pointing out how crude can be the method of communicating news of sensitive diplomatic negotiations, however, the point here lies in what Kissinger had to say in other conversations. The year 1974 was one of extensive Presidential travels abroad, first by Mr. Nixon who was trying to demonstrate he was indispensable to the conduct of foreign policy and later by Mr. Ford who was trying to demonstrate that he could conduct foreign policy. Until the last few days of the Nixon Presidency, Dr. Kissinger, as much as anyone else, beat the drums of Nixon indispensability with statements that Watergate had not weakened the administration's hand in foreign policy. In his celebrated press conference of June 11 in Salzburg, in which Kissinger said he could carry out the responsibilities of his office only "if my honor is not at issue," he was asked if the same applied to President Nixon.

"The President's position is quite different from mine," he replied. "He is an elected official. He was invited [on his trip to the Middle East] by the heads of government in a period of great transformation of international affairs and he has a duty as a President, as long as he conducts the Presidency, to conduct it in the name of the national interest and not be deflected by what may go on domestically." In Jerusalem a few days later, reporters, constantly suspecting that Watergate in fact was hampering the President in his negotiations, asked Kissinger to give something of "the tone of what goes on" in Nixon's talk with Arab and Israeli leaders. "The President's style in negotiations is a very reflective style," he said, "that is to say he does not go in there with ten specific points to bargain on a specific agreement. He believes that as President his greatest contribution is to set a general direction, to make sure the parties with whom we are dealing understand our basic purposes and then to leave to others to fill in the details of the day to day negotiations." Kissinger always left the impression that Nixon, in good times and bad, was unsurpassed as a negotiator for American interests.

His attitude was understandable. The President, whatever his strengths or weaknesses, is in charge of foreign affairs. The Secretary of State and the Presidential assistant for national security affairs—offices that Kissinger held simultaneously—answer to him. Kissinger, in order to carry out the kind of personal, free-wheeling diplomacy that he pursued needed a strong President as head of the government he represented. It was equally as understandable when Kissinger, in his rambling conversations, began to build up President Ford just as he had President Nixon. But his statements took a strange turn when he began to enhance Ford at the expense of Nixon. This started on the trip from Washington to Tokyo. Ford and Brezhnev, both gregarious, were better matched than Nixon and Brezhnev, he said, and furthermore, Ford was more interested than Nixon in the tactical side of arms talks. This was said on "deep background," which meant it was not to be attributed to anyone. The reporter would have to say it on his own. But nothing distributed to a hundred or so reporters representing news organizations around the world can stay on deep background for long, and the statement, to the surprise of no one on the White House staff, soon found its way into print, attributed to Dr. Kissinger. So did an even stronger statement Kissinger made informally to members of the Presidential party—that Ford was much more flexible than Nixon in dealing with Brezh-

nev; that Nixon never looked Brezhnev in the eye, a practice
that made the Russians suspicious; and Nixon, unlike Ford, was
arbitrary and so set in his ideas that Nixon–Brezhnev summit
meetings were difficult going. This kind of talk, which seemed
at best gratuitous, was contagious and spread like measles in a
kindergarten. After the tentative arms agreement was reached
and announced, Ron Nessen, the White House press secretary,
twice said publicly, "What Richard Nixon could not achieve in
five years, President Ford achieved in three months." This was
such nonsense—the agreement was the culmination of several
years of Nixon–Brezhnev talks—that Mr. Nessen, in a more
reflective moment back in Washington, apologized for saying it.

In retrospect, it was almost as if everyone on the trip was
playing a role, against his better judgment, acting out a stereo-
type: The Presidential assistants building up their leader larger
than life; reporters pursuing every detail of the ceremonial
aspects and angrily denouncing any official effort to cut them
out of it; the television networks directing into the homes of
millions of Americans an endless stream of color pictures of the
President, in his role as America's royalty, in exotic settings;
members of the Presidential party, men who had lived quite
ordinary lives until Gerald Ford was catapulted into the Presidency, preening in morning coats as they moved in splendor
about the official palaces; the President himself becoming so
wrapped up in it all that it apparently never occurred to him
to check the excessive statements of his aides. It was not that
everyone there did not know that excessive build-up of the
Presidency had contributed to the corruption and crisis of confidence in American government in recent years. It was as if the
excesses had become so engrained in the Presidency that it
made no difference that the office was now occupied by a plain,
unpretentious man.

On the press plane enroute home, as we all reclined in
exhaustion, Rudy Abramson of the *Los Angeles Times*, who had
recently come on the beat with a fresh eye, said, "Maybe what
we need is an emperor to go around and be celebrated and an

executive officer, like some old work-horse city manager, to run the country." Variations on this idea had been proposed for years by scholars, but at the moment it seemed extraordinarily appropriate and enticing. I don't know of any journalist who returned from that trip with any great sense of satisfaction in having explained what it was about or with the feeling the Presidency was working as it should. Imagery and substance, the phony and the real, are so inexorably intertwined in the modern White House, both on the road and at home, that even the participants frequently cannot tell the difference.

There are reporters who derive some professional satisfaction from following Dr. Kissinger around the globe but who groan at the thought of a Presidential foreign trip. Dr. Kissinger, out on his own, is himself and he conducts his business with a minimum of encumbrances. Whatever his wiles of the moment, his relationship to the press is uncomplicated. And that is the way it is with most democratic governments in the United States—the executive departments in Washington, the Congress, state houses, and city halls. No governor, mayor, senator, representative, or federal cabinet member is more than his title or his ambitions indicate, and each is continually reminded of his limitations. But the President of the United States is continually made out to be much more than the chief executive officer. There is no such thing as having a direct, uncomplicated relationship with the President. On a day to day basis, a reporter must deal not with the President but with his court. And his court can be, and frequently is, neurotic, irrational, and even contradictory. The court's chief ambition is to glorify the President, for it is in that glorification that success lies. Doing a job is frequently secondary. When an assistant such as Dr. Kissinger follows the President, he becomes part of the court and soon takes on its idiosyncrasies, without abandoning any of his own.

There is a strong temptation for the White House reporter, too, to become part of the court, to depict the President as larger than life, to assume an air of self-importance, and to view the White House as the center of the universe. It is a temptation not always resisted. For a journalist too long assigned there it can be a treacherous entrapment. It is at the same time a place of constant frustrations, large and small, and of humiliations of being herded about like cattle, and being dependent, in many respects, on a petty and capricious White House staff. Yet the news organizations never have a shortage of candidates to take on the job. Washington reporters, like politicans, are attracted to power, and in recent years the great predominance of power in the federal government has been centered in the White House.

For a period in the second Nixon term, the accumulation of Presidential powers and the pain and frustrations for reporters reached a peak at precisely the same time.

2
THE NICEST MAN IN
NORTH DAKOTA

The years 1973 and 1974 were so filled with suspense, anxiety, and enervating work for Washington journalists concerned with the national government that it was difficult many months afterwards for many of us to view the events of that period in perspective. It is like having gone through a war. What happened before seems like paled history. What happened since is so drab by comparison as to require determined concentration to follow. The cataclysm was all the more remarkable because no one, as far as I am aware, had prescience of it at the beginning of 1973. On the contrary, it seemed then we were entering a period that, as far as the national government was concerned, would be extraordinarily stuffy: a second term for Richard Nixon who appeared to have every intention of making it that way after his landslide victory in the Presidential election of 1972.

I was at home repairing the family driveway one day in late December 1972 when a call came from Clifton Daniel, the *Times'* Washington bureau manager, offering me a White House assignment. The weeks following a Presidential election has traditionally been a time of moving people into new assignments on the *Times*. R. W. Apple, Jr., who had been the chief national political reporter, already had been assigned to the White House for the beginning of the second Nixon term, but

Daniel wanted two senior reporters there in an effort to dig out news that the Nixon people were not anxious to disseminate. By that time I already had put in what I felt were two careers in journalism. The first was in Mississippi. On graduating from Emory University in Atlanta in 1949, I took my first job in journalism, at $45 a week, as reporter-editor-proofreader-headline writer and sometimes printer on the *Greenwood Morning Star*, a struggling little paper that purported to tell the news of the world and the community to a few thousand readers.

It was excellent experience for a beginner, but not the kind I would want to repeat. The *Morning Star*, now defunct, was not only short of staff, it struggled into print six days a week with some of the most decrepit mechanical equipment in the South. We never had enough headline type. The publisher, the late Virgil Adams, was as likely as not to sell an advertisement at 9 P.M. that would require some type that I already had in the chase for printing of the front page. He left me plenty of *x*'s and *z*'s but no *i*'s and *e*'s, and I would spend hours in search of synonyms that could be spelled from the diminished font. Or the linotype operator might be drunk and the next day I would get calls from amused readers wanting to know what a "peeing Tom" was. We had left out the second *p*. I endured a year and a half before moving on, but I was hooked on the newspaper business, and to this day I cannot walk into a small newspaper plant and smell the ink and grease and sweat without feeling a surge of nostalgia.

From the *Morning Star* I went to the *Jackson Daily News*, which was best known for its fire-eating editor, Frederick Sullens, then in his declining years. For decades, Sullens had kept Mississippi politics, which was unbelievably raw and gamey, in a constant state of agitation. One of his prime targets had been Senator Theodore Bilbo, not because the senator was a racial bigot—Sullens was, too—but because of some factional dispute I never quite understood. Sullens, seeking to exploit Bilbo's reputation as a womanizer, would write in his column such items as: "Senator Bilbo landed in England today while the

band played 'God Save the Queen.' " Fortunately, the news
columns were becoming a bit more objective if less fun. I flourished as a police reporter. After a few months I was made state
capitol correspondent. My salary was $55 a week and when
United Press offered me $5 more and what seemed better op-
portunities for advancement I took it. Within a short time I was
bureau manager with all of Mississippi to cover.

That was the beginning of a rather extraordinary experience. In the 1950s, the winds of social change were beginning
to blow through the South, and the news media in Mississippi,
except for a few small newspapers such as the *Greenville Delta-
Democrat Times,* published by Hodding Carter, was woefully
ill-prepared to report it. The idea of blacks as an inferior underclass which had to be kept apart was so galvanized in all of
Mississippi's dominant institutions that it was revolutionary to
think that the civil rights movement could be reported as a
legitimate force. At Emory, which was one of the centers of
liberal thought in the South, I had picked up different ideas and,
of course, the editors of UPI wanted some of the Mississippi race
story for dissemination around the world. My competition, the
Associated Press, was then dependent for news on the Heder-
man newspapers, which were committed to massive resistance
in the civil rights movement and were less than aggressive in
digging into the daily commissions of racial injustice. (The Hed-
erman family, which had long owned the *Clarion-Ledger,* acquired the *Daily News* after I left it.)

The national newspapers, magazines, and networks in the
early stages of the civil rights movement would occasionally
send in reporters, but the UPI bureau, which grew from two to
five reporters, was out front day after day in ferreting out and
reporting the lynchings, the atrocities, the resistance to change.
In the course of this, we incurred the wrath of governors, legis-
lators, sheriffs, and some newspaper editors and broadcasters
who bought our service and objected outrageously to what we
were writing. In the process, I learned one of the basics of the
news business: your freedom to write what you feel you must

rises as you meet the demand for basic news. In other words, we supplied reports on the sports scores, the traffic accidents, the murders, politics, state government, and economic development and we did it in depth and frequently first, and as a result an editor could not lightly dismiss our product. Our state report was an unconventional wire service operation. I wrote a Sunday column, which was analysis and insight more than opinion, and we carried long, in-depth stories on such subjects as the state of the state prison. Several who worked with me in those years went on to good positions in journalism. H. L. Stevenson, for one, would become the editor of UPI.

I stayed for almost a decade, much longer than I would under normal circumstances. It was a signal opportunity at a particular time in a particular place that offered what I think a journalist needs most—emersion in conflicts, in the tugs and pulls of society, whether it be a war or a social movement. I was encouraged in this by a very unusual wife, Betty, who somehow brought up four cheerful daughters despite my absences and the low level of my pay check. Together we endured the frustrations and the angry telephone calls. Ross Barnett, who became the state's stumble-bum governor in the early 1960s after several tries, would call on Saturday nights when I was in the bath tub trying to soak out the aches of the week. Betty would hand me the phone and Barnett would rant on about something I had written, while I turned on the hot water with my left foot for a long siege. When we left Mississippi in 1960 for a Nieman Fellowship at Harvard, we felt as if some of the marrow had been drawn from our bones. But there was a sense of fulfillment when we were yet young.

My second career began, I suppose, one day in July 1963 when I was in Washington helping cover the Senate for UPI. Harrison Salisbury, then the national editor of the *Times*, called from New York to ask if I was interested in going to work for the *Times*, to help Claude Sitton, the best civil rights journalist in the country, cover the exploding racial story from Atlanta. I had persuaded UPI to move me out of Mississippi, because I felt a need to move on and, like all journalists interested in government, was attracted by Washington. But after Mississippi, the Senate, although considered a choice assignment by the wire services, was dull and stultifying. So we bundled up and moved back South, where I was soon involved in the civil rights struggle as I had never been in Mississippi. One day I might be in North Carolina, covering some development there, and the next in Louisiana. I had roots in no community. I was a resident of the South, while Betty held the family together in Atlanta or Memphis, where we both were born and had family ties. But I found a home at the *Times,* which encouraged the kind of writing I had tried to do in Mississippi—the analytical approach which began from a point of view—in this case that white resistance to black moves for equality were illegal and unrealistic—and searched for deeper meanings.

I left the Southern beat after two years, just as Martin Luther King's armies were marching on Montgomery, Alabama, in the last of the great nonviolent campaigns, the protests for voting rights. If the Mississippi experience had not been so taxing for both Betty and I, we might have endured longer, for I very much liked the assignment. But we had to settle down to some kind of sensible life and the editors of the *Times* were kind enough to transfer me back to Washington. A host of new civil rights agencies and laws were being instituted and I was assigned to cover them, in Washington and occasionally out in the country. Later, I helped cover national politics, Congress and urban affairs, the latter a beat that involved national travel and gave me a broadened education in the country and its people. In the 1972 elections, I jumped at the opportunity to cover national issues, a story that fizzled because the only issue in the Presidential race was that of personalities.

As 1972 drew to a close, I was feeling a sense of weariness and uncertainty about what I should do. I had brought to journalism a strong sense of optimism that most white Americans of my generations shared. My father had been a small-town merchant in west Tennessee and although we never had

enough income to feel secure, there was always the feeling—
growing in part, I think, out of the Christian faith that I em-
braced at an early age—that tomorrow would be better. But in
1972, my memory was a panaroma of shattering events. I had
seen too much of tragedy and violence. I had known and respected Medgar Evers, the Mississippi civil rights leader who
was shot down in cold blood by a warped segregationist; I could
not get out of my head the scene of the Sixteenth Street Baptist
Church in Birmingham minutes after four young girls were
bombed to death; I had spent three weeks in Dallas after the
assasination of President Kennedy; I had seen his brother, Robert F. Kennedy, lying in his own blood in the Ambassador Hotel
kitchen in Los Angeles after I had covered his short but intense
Presidential campaign in 1968; I had known Martin Luther
King, Jr., well and heard repeatedly his forebodings of early
death before he was finally assassinated in Memphis; I had seen
innocent but brave people beaten, brutalized, or killed in small
towns across the South; I had seen the civil rights movement,
with its theme of universal love, turn now and splinter away to
nothing; I had seen the black sections of the nation's cities go
up in smoke and violence; I had covered the Presidential commissions that searched for the causes of violence and hatred; I
had seen the naïve children of the 1950s, who wanted quick
justice, beaten in the streets in the 1960s by the police in
Chicago and other cities, until they, too, turned violent; I had
seen much of the white middle class, which I had thought of as
generous, turn cynical and cold and indifferent to the needs of
the unfortunate at home and abroad. I had to keep reminding
myself that the pictures in my head distorted reality, that the
country was much more than that.

Out of all of my experiences, I had come to have a strong
empathy for the underclass, and developed a skepticism of high
officials everywhere. I felt that an adversary relationship was
the only right one between a reporter and government officials.
I mistrusted, perhaps too much, people who were very smart
and were educated in the best schools but who had no scar

tissue from the conflicts of life, and Washington is filled with these.

In assessing what I should do as 1973 approached, I had expressed an interest, among other things, in the White House, because of the challenge it represented. Like the proverbial mountain, it was there, tough and foreboding, a peak seldom scaled in the proper manner, I thought, by the succession of journalists in the Kennedy–Johnson–Nixon years. Yet the thought of it, once assigned, left me in doubt that was not to be dispelled in my first days on the job. When I informed James Deakin of the *St. Louis Post-Dispatch*, who had covered the place since Eisenhower, that I was joining him he said, "You must have drawn the low number in the office pool."

The humor that bubbles up occasionally through the cynicism in the White House press room is, on many days, all that makes that small compound bearable. It is a compound in more than a figurative sense, because it is the only place in the White House and the adjacent Executive Office Building where reporters can go and come at will. The reporter may enter the grounds by showing his Secret Service pass, and walk without challenge through the door of the West Wing that opens to the briefing room. From there he can roam the two small rooms where desks and telephones are set up for reporters and the suite of offices where the press secretary and his assistants work. Entry to any other area requires an appointment and an escort. If there is a ceremony in the East Room, the Oval Office, or the Rose Garden that is open to coverage, reporters and photographers are herded there en masse; and if one has an appointment to interview an official, he is met by a secretary who ushers him quickly through the mysterious halls to the proper office.

Formerly the press room had been in the West Wing lobby. President Nixon, in his first term, had it moved to nearby space that for many years had been the Presidential swimming pool. The reason given was that the press needed more space, and the new area did provide larger and better quarters. However, some reporters suspected an ulterior motive, a suspicion subsequently confirmed by Alexander P. Butterfield, who had been a Nixon assistant at the time, in testimony in the summer of 1974 before the House Judiciary Committee. The President, he said, decided to "get the press out of the west lobby, so they would not inhibit guests to the White House and bother them." By putting the press in the swimming pool area, he explained, reporters and photographers not only were cut off from the goings and comings of White House visitors but from the suites of offices used by the top Presidential aides.

The new quarters also enhanced the salesmanship techniques employed by the Nixon administration. A blue curtain was hung behind the podium of the briefing room to enhance the television image of Press Secretary Ronald L. Ziegler and others who appeared there from time to time. Loud speakers planted somewhere in the rooms brought announcements from time to time of events that could be covered, contributing to the "big brother" atmosphere of the place. "There will be a photo opportunity in the Oval Office." This meant photographers could go in and take pictures of the President meeting with some dignitary. Photographers are tough, no-nonsense people and the phrase "photo opportunity," substituted for their term, "picture session," disgusted them, but the press office could never pass up the chance to make it appear that those covering the White House were being done a favor. On the walls of the offices open to reporters, clusters of stars that can be lighted individually were installed. The stars are coded somehow—so many lighted or not lighted, for example, means no more announcements for the day. During two years there on a daily basis, I never did learn the code. I tried not to notice the stars, perhaps out of a dread of being programmed. I don't know.

Even in the Executive Office Building, that magnificent old Victorian structure at the corner of Pennsylvania Avenue and Seventeenth Street, entry is only by appointment. Frequently the guards who sit stoically at each entrance do not receive the word for clearance for those who have an appointment, and the visitors are kept fuming in the lobby until the matter is worked out. In this barricaded institution comprising the two buildings and called the Executive Office of the President, scores of faceless officials sit in spacious offices making decisions that affect millions, seeing only those they want to see from the outside and protected by telephone by competent, highly paid secretaries who collect and stack the calls that are answered only if the official so chooses. I know of no other government institution in the United States, with the exception of intelligence agencies, so insulated from the public. The stated purpose is to insure the people and buildings against possible violence, yet in those guarded halls, members of the President's staff are free to carry out their intrigues and inside conflicts that occur in one degree or another in every administration.

This insularity and segregation contributes to the *them vs. us* feeling that is so strong among officials and reporters in the White House. Under President Nixon, at the beginning of 1973, that feeling was particularly intense. The President had gone into a period of depression after his landslide reelection—the best explanation for this, derived from his book, *Six Crises,* was that he felt best at the height of a crisis but let down and blue after a victory—and was spending most of his time at Camp David brooding and preparing for his second term. Although about 80 percent of the nation's newspapers had supported Mr. Nixon for reelection, he had begun, through his assistants, systematic punishment of those who had offended him. News of the appointments and resignations were leaked to the friendly *Washington Star-News* to punish its competitor, the unfriendly *Washington Post.* If *Time* Magazine published a story less than favorable to the administration, White House aides would grant an interview to *Newsweek*, *Time*'s competitor, or vice versa. Mostly, however, White House aides, with the exception of Dr. Kissinger, talked to no one in the news business, except in the regular press briefings or on television to make a hard sell for Richard Nixon.

For most Americans there is a compelling mystique about

the White House that stands out above all else in Washington, and this feeling is shared even by that band of cynical journalists who have a long-worn familiarity with the place. We were educated that way. Two generations of Presidential scholars, their thoughts penetrating classrooms and textbooks, succeeded in planting in the minds of millions the idea that the last best hope for prosperity, justice, and the realization of the national dream rested primarily in the Presidency, the office that represents all of the people, the one best equipped in modern times to take the initiative and get things done. Here the institution is a person who can be blamed, petitioned, celebrated, and over the years public attention has been increasingly focused on the holder of the office, his family, and subordinates. The physical surroundings in which he lives and works add to the aura of importance, of being at the center of power. Perhaps more than any other building in Washington, the columned White House, with its graceful lines and spacious lawns and gardens, evokes the eighteenth-century origins of the national government reason, balance, and symmetry.

The mystique is nurtured with constant care in our age of disorder and complexity. No crabgrass or dandelion intrudes on the lawn. No dead wood remains in the giant elms. No flower fades before it is replaced by another with fresh color. No crack survives in the smooth-surfaced driveways. No smudge remains on a windowpane. No worn or peeled paint is tolerated. A suite is redecorated overnight at the whim of the occupant to suit his individual taste. The gardeners, the servants, the guards, the secretaries, the functionaries are the most efficient and obedient in the government. Everything related to comfort and convenience works for the President and his assistants. American history is idealized in the portraits, busts, and art that decorate historic rooms and halls. A Presidential assistant, seated behind a desk in a spacious office with banks of telephones, television sets, secretaries, servants, and much of the enormous federal bureaucracy at his command, acquires a sense of power and majesty. For the visitor, it is like stepping from one world into another when he leaves the public streets of the District of Columbia and is inside the White House grounds. And this is partly why for some, who have long been there, the view of life and reality from the Presidential compound is seldom like that which prevails outside.

For a White House reporter, it is necessary first of all to acquire a feel for the President, his character, his motivations, his views of the office and the country, and the manner in which he deals with his assistants and others. In January 1973, Richard Nixon was to me a distant and enigmatic figure as seen backwards through a telescope. During his first term he had rarely made himself available for interviews, background sessions or informal chats that Presidents traditionally had used as a means of projecting themselves favorably to the public. Because of his long-held dislike and distrust of the Washington press corps he had made a hard decision in his first term to by-pass the White House press and make his appeal directly to the nation through television, radio, and through his office of communications, a supplementary White House press office that dealt directly with editors, broadcasters, and other opinion makers. Having succeeded at this in the 1972 election, it was apparent that in his second term he would be even more remote.

I had known Richard Nixon in 1966, when I was assigned to him for two weeks when he was flying about the country speaking in behalf of Republican candidates for Congress. He was making a comeback after his angry departure from politics following his 1962 defeat in the California governor's race, and was laying the groundwork for the 1968 Presidential election. He was effective in his campaigning and was unlike the Richard Nixon I had read about through the years. I tried to reflect this in my copy. In one story I began, "You couldn't find a nicer man in all of North Dakota today than Richard M. Nixon." He kissed babies. At press conferences he displayed humility. He criss-crossed the country in a slow, two-engine Convair, accompanied only by his secretary, Rose Mary Woods, a handful of associates who volunteered to help him out, and a reporter or two. He talked to me at length in a kind of avuncular way. He told me how he was trying to keep the right wing of the party in line. When I asked him questions on farm policy he said, "I have found the only way to appeal to the farmer is to sit on the tail gate of a pickup truck with him and help him complain." He inquired about my ambitions and my family and later sent an autographed copy of *Six Crises* to my oldest daughter, Claudia.

But that was the last personal contact I had with him, and his first term in the Presidency had reaffirmed all my old Nixon prejudices. During that period I was not concerned with foreign policy, his forte and center of interest, but urban affairs and the fate of the nation's underclass. His approach to social domestic programs was so cynical and so insensitive to the real needs of people, I thought, that he had done inestimatible damage to the fragile beginnings of social justice in this country. On school desegregation, for example, his ambiguous white papers paying lip service to the concept of integrated education while opposing busing in the most simplistic kind of way were infuriating to those who had a feel for the subject. It was not that there was not a legitimate argument to be made against long-distance busing. It was that the President of the United States, with responsibility for representing all of the people, knew all too well the politics of school desegregation and was using the issue for reelection in 1972, while he seemed to have no interest or understanding of the substance of what was involved in this great civil rights struggle that over the years had produced a body of law based on basic constitutional rights. In a larger sense, he seemed totally unconcerned for the millions of poor in the decaying central cities while he catered to the most selfish motives of the affluent majority in the suburban ring.

In fairness to the Nixon White House, I must confess I was not prepared to be easily converted to the idea, then current in some circles, that President Nixon, having won a second term by so wide a margin and unable to succeed himself, would be generous and anxious to bind the nation's wounds in his last four years in office. No one in the White House seemed inclined to convey that impression. Every bit of evidence that emerged from the White House that winter reflected a state of mind that was hard, cold, and combative. In 1969, when Mr. Nixon had been inaugurated for his first term, he called for governmental pursuit of full employment, better housing, excellence in education, and rebuilding the cities. In his 1973 inaugural, he said the nation must forego the "false promise" of government solutions for domestic problems, and he urged citizens to "ask not just what government will do for me, but what can I do for myself." This stern approach was conveyed to the press by John D. Ehrlichman, Mr. Nixon's chief adviser on domestic affairs, who stood before the blue curtain in the press room and told reporters that Congress, in proposing spending for domestic programs beyond the President's budget, was, in reality, preparing a series of "trojan horses" for the White House, the center of enlightenment.

Preparations for combat were being made on several fronts. A reorganization of the executive branch was underway that would permit the President to control the bureaucracy; programs enacted by law would be phased out by executive order through impoundment of congressionally appropriated funds; in several ways the White House would seek to expand Presidential powers, in both domestic and foreign areas, at the expense of the legislative and judicial branches. These preparations seemed all the more ominous because they coincided with the Christmas bombing of North Vietnamese cities. Acting without the advice of either the Congress or the Joint Chiefs of Staff, an isolated and brooding President extorted from a small country the dubious peace settlement that brought the President almost a 70 percent approval rating in the public opinion polls. In every respect, the Nixon spokesmen said, the President was acting out of his 1972 mandate.

All of this put a tremendous burden on Ronald Ziegler's press office, which was required to deny that the administration was doing anything out of the ordinary and to maintain with dead seriousness that it was an open Presidency, and on the reporters who had to depend on the Ziegler briefings almost exclusively for White House news. Although the daily White House news briefing, which is a strange institution in any administration, was not new to me, I was not prepared for the tension and surreal quality I found there in 1973.

At thirty-four years of age, Ziegler had survived four years in one of the toughest jobs in Washington. The President and almost everyone in the official White House gave him high marks for the way he handled the press, putting out exactly what the President and his staff wanted, and no more, and he ran an efficient office, which meant that the media had quick and easy access to that which was released. The mimeograph machines ran on time. If Ziegler minded conveying only what he was told to convey—and we know from the White House tapes he was a willing part of the regime—he never showed it. He was quite sure of himself in those days, very authoritative and very maddening to the reporter whose job was to know what was going on in the closed corridors and offices.

An example of the Ziegler performance was the following exchange regarding reports that James Rowley, then head of the White House Secret Service, was under pressure to retire because a Secret Service agent had offended H. R. Haldeman, the White House chief of staff, in insisting on certain security precautions for the President on a trip to Providence, Rhode Island.

QUESTION: There was a report in *The New York Times* earlier this week about a confrontation between Robert Taylor and H. R. Haldeman in Providence; a quarrel, reported by the *Times*, about letting crowds in. How do you square that report with your statement that there is no rift between these two gentlemen?

MR. ZIEGLER: We are going to keep this story running and running and running, aren't we, even after Rowley's statement. If we keep it up, maybe we can go for ten or fifteen days. Every time I comment on it, it is another story. I will stand on my initial comment

and I will stand on what Director Rowley said yesterday. As director
of the Secret Service, he addressed that subject specifically and it
correlates entirely with what I am saying.

QUESTION: Are you denying the Providence report?

MR. ZIEGLER: Here it goes. Here is another story. Yes, I am.
"The White House denied today that . . ." So there is five days on a story
that has no basis in fact to it.

QUESTION: Is Jim Rowley retiring, Ron?

MR. ZIEGLER: No, he is not, not to my knowledge.

The incident was forgotten in the rush of other, more significant disclosures about Mr. Haldeman. A few weeks later
Rowley quietly retired. Whether the reports were true or not
is beside the point. The point here is that I do not know of a
reporter who believed Ziegler's disclaimers.

On the other hand, some reporters made a ceremony of
talking tough to Ziegler, a tact that seemed to have no effect in
eliciting information. Some of the tough talk, in fact, came from
reporters who never wrote tough copy, either by their own
inclination or because of restraints their organizations placed
on them. In some instances, they preached sermons in their
questions for the benefits of Presidential assistants, perhaps
even the President, who were known to read the transcripts of
the briefings or to listen to it on "the squawk box." The White
House press, as a group, suffered a neurosis from living under
constant frustration. Some of the tough talk and sermonizing
was simply to serve notice that the daily obfuscation by the
official White House would not be accepted without protest.

I was not interested in making speeches for the record, or
taking on Ziegler in the briefings. The thought of having to rely
only on White House official pronouncements for my stories left
me in some despair. It soon became apparent that if the White
House were to be covered with any sense of competence I
would have to employ techniques far different from any I had
used on the many and assorted beats I had covered in the past.

3
A BEAT
WITHOUT SOURCES

One difficulty with White House reporting is that we are daily victims of our own devices. The media, having built up the Presidency over the years out of proportion to its constitutional importance and having encouraged its seizures of power, frequently find ourselves feeding the voracious appetite of the Presidency, both out of habit and necessity. No other institution can demand space and attention throughout the media when there is no news there. The White House does every day. The President can demand front-page coverage by holding a press conference in which he says nothing that has not been said before. He can command prime television time by granting an exclusive interview to one of the networks, and newspapers feel compelled to write about it at length because millions saw it on television. The White House press secretary knows, before he knows hardly anything else, that the President can grab the headlines on a quiet day by making a ceremonial appearance or overshadowing Congress or his political opponents by some act or statement that is sure to command the greater amount of attention.

The press secretary has all kinds of devices for manipulating the media. He can release a statement of dubious integrity and have it run almost without challenge, simply by making it available, say, on a Saturday afternoon when all of the departments and agencies which could contribute to the subject are closed and the reporter specialists who know the subject are off duty. White House reporters are by necessity generalists who cannot possibly know all of the complex subjects before the federal government. Too frequently, in order to make a deadline or out of too much trust in the White House press office, the White House correspondent will report information that is wrong or misleading with no attempt to put it in focus.

In an exalted institution, the reporter can gain access to news by gaining the trust of those inside. But frequently this means serving the source's purpose before his own. When a Presidential assistant wants to leak some news, he will do so to a reporter whom he believes will use it as it is put out with the least amount of checking and balancing. The reporter will win accolades from his organization for his exclusive and soon be back for more. If the White House wants to float a "trial balloon," a statement of intention to see if the public will buy a proposal, the reporter too often is the willing tool simply because his source is authoritative and highly placed.

For years, it was the practice of the press office to suggest privately to a particular reporter a question that the President would like to respond to in a press conference, and the reporter more often than not would ask it in order to produce news or win the favor of the White House. Several years ago, one reporter who had had a string of exclusive stories from White House sources was requested by a press officer to ask a certain question. He took umbrage at the suggestion, saying he would not ask a "planted question." The press officer, stung by the rebuke, asked if he had the same feeling about "planted answers." It was a good point. Exclusive stories, except when a reporter digs into a particular subject to find answers, usually are planted by some official who has some reason, perhaps self-serving, for wanting them published. The source usually expects something in return, if nothing more than favorable treatment for himself in the news columns. It is rare indeed that news is leaked out of public interest.

These devices of manipulation have been used at all levels of government over the years, but they are particularly pronounced at the White House because of the concentration of authority there and because of the arrogance that power breeds in people. In the Kennedy–Johnson–Nixon years, manipulation of the press, many of us in journalism thought, had reached an extreme.

In January 1973, the White House press was under criticism from several quarters for yeilding too easily to this manipulation and for not being aggressive enough in finding out what happened in the Watergate scandals. President Nixon was able to make a successful race for reelection without having to account, in any detailed way, for the Watergate burglary which his agents had committed. It was true, he rarely subjected himself to questioning, either in a press conference or otherwise. But when the opportunity did arise, the reporters did not dig in, as they were to do later, with extensive questioning, and in the 1972 election, millions of people went to the polls with the calm assurance of the President that no one at the White House was involved in the scandal. Nor did anyone in the White House press find out prior to the election about all the scheming and conniving that was going on behind the scenes.

Although I was not at the White House or working on the Watergate story at the time, I am convinced from hindsight and subsequent experience that the press could and should have pressed Mr. Nixon harder on Watergate. But I also am convinced that the White House press room is the last place from which to launch a journalistic investigation of crime and corruption. If there is anyone in those sheltered offices and halls who would choose to expose his colleagues or hand out damaging documents surreptitiously, a White House reporter probably is the last person he would trust, because of the interplay of reporters and officials within the institution and thus the risk of the reporter's source becoming known to his colleagues and superiors. Further, a White House reporter's prime job is to find out and report what kind of government the President is presiding over and what is the quality and direction of his leadership. There is little time for painstaking research into reported wrongdoing. That is the job for the investigative reporter working from the outside.

A generation of Washington journalists, now in middle age, grew up under the belief that both the federal government and journalism had matured, that people in the federal government were trustworthy within reasonable limits and would not steal the Capitol dome or overthrow the democratic institutions, and that journalists could best be of public service by requiring a sophisticated knowledge of policies and politics. If the people were to be done in, it was believed, it would be through subtle legislation or executive action or leadership that favored classes or individuals. The catch-the-crooks school of newspapering that had flourished early in the century was long dead except in isolated places. Yet Washington, in the 1970s, had to reinvent the old-time police reporter. They are young, most of them, but they are right out of Chicago journalism of the 1920s and 1930s in their techniques. The best of them have mysterious sources, they threaten, they flatter, they trade information, they deal with an underground of rumor and gossip as they follow one thread after another to catch the crooks. It is marvelous to listen to them on the telephone. Without them, the stories that began the process of disclosure of the Watergate scandals by the prosecutors, the courts, and Congress would never have appeared.

Their success in no way invalidated the need for the policy-political types. Rather, it demonstrated the need for diversity in the Washington media. If there was fault to be found with the policy-political reporting, it was the failure to convey to the country the character of the people in charge of the government. It did not require the disclosure of a White House enemy's list to document that there was a siege mentality at work that was a threat to democratic government. It did not require evidence of White House involvement in the Watergate burglary or the Presidential tape recordings to document that there was massive deception at work. It was all around us. There were the publicized incidents including, among others, the summary firing of Interior Secretary Walter Hickel and a number of other lesser officials when they sought to be adversaries within the administration; the assignment of FBI agents to investigate Daniel Schorr, the television correspondent, when he broadcasted a story the President's aides did not like, then sought to cover it up with the lie that Schorr was being considered for a federal job; the refusal of Nixon to campaign and submit to questioning in the 1972 Presidential campaign in disregard of tradition. But there also were incidents barely noticed in the media that would have supported the theme that this administration was an aberration from what Americans expected of democratic government. In communities where Nixon made public appearances there were a host of examples of the excessive use of police force to control the crowds so as to show Nixon popularity; in some cities those who had sought to carry anti-Nixon signs took legal action against the government after being mauled by police acting under the direction of White House agents. There were numerous examples of the cult on the Nixon staff which held that next to personal loyalty to Nixon the standard for excellence was the ability to do in the Nixon enemies; after Ken W. Clawson, a *Washington Post* reporter, was brought onto the staff despite the fears of some that he might leak news to his former colleagues, the word got around that Clawson was a gut fighter ready to take on the "Eastern press" and all other enemies, and he soon became a member of the cult. And so on. But we all were too little sensitive to it, perhaps out of having grown too comfortable in official Washington, too trusting of the institutions. Of course, there was some excellent reporting that described what it was all about, but it was the exception rather than the rule and was never massive enough to make much of an impression on the American people.

My own feeling about White House reporting of the past was that both the print and the broadcast media carried too much too prominently of what the President said or did, whether or not it had much meaning. It was carried simply because he was the President. And this, in turn, encouraged Americans to look to that office for the answers to public policy, whether or not the President carried the authority necessary to act in the area of concern. On almost any day—in rain, shine, sleet or snow—there are pickets on Pennsylvania Avenue making a symbolic appeal to the President for some cause. Antipornography groups, for example, picket the White House rather than the Supreme Court, which has jurisdiction in that area. I have seen workers who demand wage legislation petition the White House but never go to Congress, even though that was where their chief opposition lay. The belief that the President can do anything continues to be supported by the media through the constant barrage of publicity given to him and his assistants. Yet the White House reporter who may be concerned about this, frequently finds himself powerless to do much because White House activity has so long been defined as top news that the demand by his editors and the need to be competitive compel him to keep pouring out the copy.

One solution to this, I thought in the first weeks of my assignment, would be to produce more copy critical of the institution and less that stated what the President did or said without raising any underlying questions. The ideal way to do this for a large organization such as the *Times* would be to divide the White House among specialists who would cover the President and his appropriate aides on a particular subject. The foreign affairs specialist, for example, could then balance the statements coming out of the White House on foreign policy against his own knowledge and what he learns from the State Department. The same would apply for, say, the labor reporter, or the reporter for science and health, and so on to as many as twenty subjects. I had long been convinced that institutional reporting—the assignment of a reporter to a place such as Congress, a department, or the White House—was inadequate, though sometimes necessary. Not only are the many matters government is concerned with highly complex and frequently confusing, but statements by government officials simply cannot be taken on faith. Lying and distortion, consciously or unconsciously, out of good motives and bad, have become so much a part of the fabric of official Washington that much of what is said is, or should be, suspect.

Years of covering civil rights and urban affairs had impressed this on me. On housing, I had found that to write about it from the standpoint of the public interest required an extensive knowledge of the subject. All of the chief institutions involved—the Federal Housing Administration, the congressional committees in charge of housing legislation, the building and lending associations—were either corrupt or under the undue influence of special interests, or both. Each of these organizations bring influence to bear on the White House, which in its actions and pronouncements must always show it is acting in the public interest. For a novice on the subject of housing to write about what the White House does or says about the matter is an almost certain way to mislead the public. Yet this happens every day on a wide range of subjects.

On March 21, 1973, President Nixon said in a statement that he was pleased to report that $424 million in federal funds would be made available in the summer for 776,000 public service jobs for youths. The statement went on to say that the outlook for youths in the coming summer was encouraging. Overall it sounded like a very generous act on the part of the government to offset the chronically high unemployment rate among young people during the summer. Most of the dispatches reported it that way.

Only because of my experience in urban affairs reporting did I become suspicious about a portion of the statement which said the bulk of the funds, $300 million, would come out of money appropriated for the Emergency Employment Assistance Act, which was enacted to provide year-round public service jobs, mostly for adults, and it would be up to local officials to decide whether to use the $300 million for adults or youths.

Under the laws then current, summer youth jobs were to be funded under a separate act. Informed of the President's statement, Senator Jacob K. Javits, Republican of New York, exploded: "Cities are left with the Hobson's choice of firing the father in order to hire the son." It was a classic case of the White House acting in an calculated manner, then making it appear otherwise.

To a certain extent, the White House has been covered by specialists, particularly on foreign policy and economics. But this is difficult to do on a day to day basis. The President and his assistants are frequently out of town and it is not possible to have twenty reporters from one organization following him around or even attending the daily news briefings in Washington. Further, shortly after arriving on the beat, I saw that the Presidency under Nixon was a specialized subject that would be a long time in the news and require a special expertise.

Shortly after Nixon was inaugurated for a second term, reports from Washington of how he was consolidating his authority grew so numerous that the *Times'* managing editor, A. M. Rosenthal, asked for some special stories defining what it was all about, and I gladly took on the assignment. R. W. Apple, Jr. and I were sharing the White House beat, at that time, one of us attending to the routine of daily briefings and handouts, while the other roamed around looking for more meaningful material. Using my time away from the routine, I started investigating Presidential powers by going through the normal channels. I went to see Ronald Ziegler in his office. It was a high-ceilinged room with large, formal windows looking out on Pennsylvania Avenue. Ziegler sat behind a curved desk with a telephone console at his side. There were three television sets, one for each network, pictures of the President, himself, and other White House dignitaries on the wall. In an anteroom two wire service teletypes ticked away in a soundproof box while three secretaries typed busily and answered telephones. This was the inner sanctum of the press office. The main body of personnel dealing directly with the press held forth in tighter quarters off the blue-curtained briefing room.

Because the story I was at work on was going to be of some importance, I asked Ziegler if it would be possible that the President himself might like to say a few words on the subject? He looked at me as if he thought I was crazy, shook his head and said, "No chance." I suppose by that time Ziegler knew to whom the President would or would not talk and knew when it was useless to try. But this was a subject of some sensitivity for the President and I thought Ziegler was a little too eager to dismiss my request. He ticked off a list of people he thought I should see, quickly gave me his own views on the subject and indicated it was time for me to go. He was a very busy man.

Of the White House officials Ziegler named, I felt it was absolutely essential that I see Ehrlichman, the President's chief domestic adviser, who also was a lawyer, and was known to have some conceptual thoughts about how the institution should work. It has long been hard to get to high officials in Washington. They are eternally in meetings and, because so many people are demanding their time, they are surrounded by secretaries who take it on themselves to screen their bosses from intrusion.

There was no rush to see Ehrlichman and the others I called, however. Anytime in the next two weeks would be fine, I told their secretaries, informing them of the subject matter and the fact that it would be a major story, or stories, in the *Times*. They would call me, they promised, when something could be worked out. In the meantime, I visited Congress and toured the country, interviewing anyone I could find who had knowledge of Presidential authority and some insights to what Nixon was about. It was like tapping a geyser. Enough facts and opinions to make a major case of extensive abuse of power flowed out to fill several books. Scholars, with their long view of history, could put it in perspective. Henry Steele Commager, the historian, sat in the library of his 1840s house outside Amherst, Massachusetts, one February day and said more in thirty minutes than could be obtained in Washington in weeks.

"He has usurped or aggrandized authority in almost every field," Dr. Commager said, as he gazed alternately at the snowy meadows outside his window and at the shelves of worn books that reached to the ceiling. "Even in wartime—the only thing comparable is the Civil War, which was a very special kind of war and therefore the kind of instantaneous action that Lincoln took was domestically required—even in wartime, it seems to me there was no such broad-gauged and wide-fronted assault on the constitutional integrity of the constitutional system as we now have." President Lincoln, he said, "did not try to undermine the court, for example, as Mr. Nixon is undermining the court. He did not challenge the power of Congress over appropriations as Mr. Nixon is doing. He did not exert executive prerogatives and executive privileges as Mr. Nixon is doing, not only for himself but for subordinates well down the line. In so many ways, I think, Mr. Nixon has gone far beyond any previous President in our history."

Not everyone I talked to was of so strong an opinion as Dr. Commager, but there was almost unanimous opinion that Nixon was taking the national government into uncharted waters. In the meantime, my requests for interviews with White House officials drew few responses. Ehrlichman, whom I had known from my days of covering urban affairs, never did respond, even though I called his secretary several times. I had to settle for rather low-level people who did not seem to comprehend the subject. It was just as well. My stories ran on the front page as a series for four consecutive days beginning Sunday, March 3, without the ambiguity there might have been if the White House had chosen to refute my conclusions and given me statements that we would have had to include out of fairness. But the series did not win me any sources.

Thereafter, I was faced by stark reality: The Nixon White House had little interest in the standard public relations practice of influencing as much as possible what goes in the media. The President and his assistants apparently had given up on papers like *The New York Times,* however influential, and would instruct the public in his own way—through direct television and radio appearances and whatever media that was considered friendly to the White House. Where there was access, there was very rarely any useful information imparted by the officials. It was a beat without sources. Other than reporting official acts and statements, with whatever interpretation I could muster, covering the White House became a matter of trying to perceive through sight and sound what was happening and build stories on that perception. To my surprise, it turned out to be more reliable than any official word from those strange men who held Washington in their grip.

4
DOWN ON THE PLANTATION

Every morning, the reporters would gather to await the 11 A.M. briefing. The announcement from the loud-speaker, "there will be a briefing in the briefing room," usually was a long time coming, sometimes two hours or more after the scheduled time. The explanation was that the press secretary simply could not get everything together any sooner on a particular day. However, if the reporter should decide to wait until, say, twelve noon to show up, it was likely that the briefing would have started on time. So a good part of most days was taken up waiting for the briefing. It was useless to try to work or do much reading in the atmosphere of clutter and confusion in the crowded room. Even use of the telephone was limited because every word spoken could be heard by a number of people. In lighter moments, a raconteur such as Peter Lisagore of the *Chicago Daily News* or Hugh Sidey of Time-Life might hold forth with Lyndon Johnson stories or other ribald tales. But usually the talk centered on exchanges of opinion about the President and his assistants. By the time I arrived at the White House, the talk was almost totally negative.

It was not only the lack of access to information and the fact that most reporters had an unfavorable opinion of the Nixon regime; those who had been there for some time felt that they had been abused—not so much personally, as in the sense that legitimate functions of the press had been manipulated and in a way that the reporters were powerless to prevent. Thus the gripe sessions had a tone of paranoia about them. If the Nixon people had a siege mentality at a time when there was no evidence to show they were under serious threat from their enemies, real and imagined, the White House press had grievances that could be documented. My impression after sitting through a few of those sessions was that the reporters reminded me of peons on a plantation sitting in quarters off-hours complaining of the overseer or others in the big house who controlled their lives in their proscribed world of work.

The White House press is diverse and the needs and political ideology of its members vary widely. Newspapers assigning reporters full time to the White House include *The New York Times*, the *Washington Post*, the *Washington Star-News*, the *Chicago Tribune*, the *Chicago Daily News*, the *St. Louis Post-Dispatch*, the *Baltimore Sun*, the *Los Angeles Times*, Scripps-Howard newspapers, Hearst newspapers, the *Wall Street Journal*, the *Philadelphia Bulletin*, Newhouse newspapers, and others whose reporters work from cubbyholes in the rectangular room over the cavity that was the swimming pool and who travel with the President whenever he is out of town. Other newspapers send their bureau chiefs when there is something of special interest to them going on at the White House.

Each of the two domestic wire services, Associated Press and United Press International, has a small, soundproof office at the end of the larger room and three reporters assigned full time to the White House. Reuters, the English-based wire service, and Agency France Press, have one reporter each assigned to the President. They work out of cubbyholes alongside the newspaper reporters.

The major broadcast networks, which have three or four reporters each at the White House, and smaller networks such as Group W Radio and Golden West Radio occupy small broadcast booths at the end of the press room, or downstairs at what was the bottom of the swimming pool. The news magazines—

Time, Newsweek, U. S. News, the *New Republic*—and other periodicals are assigned to the lower level. Photographers, camermen and technicians complete the group of seventy or so assigned regularly to cover the President—a wide assortment, so different in their interests and motivations that I never knew them to form a unanimous opinion on anything except the need for access.

To perform his job, the White House reporter must have a degree of access. As the President goes about governing the country, even if he is an enigma, the reporter must at least have some signs of his behavior and thinking, some small clues to follow in framing his explanation of what the President is all about. It is no longer adequate in journalism, if it ever was, simply to report what the President and his assistants say and do in their official acts and appearances. Almost any literate person can do that in an organized fashion. The reason for sending an experienced reporter to the White House is so that he will provide insights and information that are not generally available.

In any administration the press secretary is in a position of the plantation overseer. He is the person the reporter must deal with on a day to day basis. He can punish or reward by providing or prohibiting access. One of the rewards under a seclusive President is to be on the pools where important things happen. On Air Force One, for example, it is possible to obtain insights and bits of information that do not come through in the pool report. A reporter on the pool that follows the President to the speaking rostrum can get a better view of how the President looks and behaves, who he talks to and what his mood is. Under Nixon, this was very important, because of the enormous pressures he was under and his tendency to seclude himself.

The assignment of pools is done by organization rather than individuals. The two wire services are assigned to all pools because of their need to provide quick blanket coverage of everything that happens, although they very rarely provide insight because of the standards of objectivity imposed on their reporters and the rush to get the news on the wire. The others —the newspapers, the newsmagazines and the broadcasters who assign people full time to the White House—are supposed to be assigned to pools, on a rotation basis, as they come up. But it has rarely worked that way. The press secretary or his assistants vary the assignments for any number of arbitrary reasons. In other words, he uses the assignment power to achieve his own end.

With Ron Ziegler, I discovered, the assignments followed a pattern. Reporters who wrote harsh copy about the White House seldom, if ever, were assigned to important pools. How much of this was Ziegler's idea and how much was directed from above I was never able to determine. I do know that a sure way to get stricken from the good pools was to write something that put Mr. Ziegler's press office in bad light. If Ziegler heard that a reporter was about to write something about him or his operation, he would call the reporter in for a little chat, a check to see what was on the reporter's mind and, I thought, to let the reporter know he was being watched. I had always been offended by the precedent of the press secretary summoning a reporter to see him rather than his going to the reporter when he had something to complain about.

In 1968, while covering the Robert Kennedy Presidential campaign, I was filling in one day for the regular White House reporter, Max Frankel, when I heard myself being summoned on the loud-speaker to appear in the office of George Christian, President Johnson's last press secretary. I stood at the desk while Christian, who was as fair and mild as anyone who served in that office in recent years, enumerated to me all the errors he thought I had made in a story I had written on a meeting between Johnson and Kennedy, two long-time antagonists. I had quoted Kennedy sources and done all I could to get the Johnson side of the meeting and I did not believe I owed Christian any explanation. It was the idea of being summoned to stand accused that offended me. This was part of the aggrandizement of the Presidency. "You are writing about the President of the United States!" Christian said.

In 1974, after Ziegler had taken on the role of confidant to the President and had turned over the daily briefings to Gerald L. Warren, his deputy, it became increasingly difficult to see Ziegler or reach him on the telephone. I remember one period of several days when Ziegler did not return my telephone calls, even though he held the title as press secretary and I covered the White House for the newspaper that most people considered the most influencial in the United States. It seemed an appropriate time to do a story on what was happening to the press office, and I began interviewing people in preparation for the story. Ziegler found out what I was doing and sent word he wanted to see me. He made no mention of the unanswered telephone calls but said quite frankly he had heard I was writing a story on the press office and wanted to make sure I was not getting any false impressions of internal disputes and such. The insensitivity to what the *Times'* needs might be and the over-sensitivity to White House public relations was consistent, I thought, with the spirit of the Ziegler operation throughout.

There was a convenient means of keeping unfriendly reporters off the good pools short of outright violation of the rotation system. The press office would wait until the reporter was taking a few days off before assigning his organization to the pool. The spot would then be filled by a substitute reporter, who had no special interest or knowledge of the White House and who had no need to store insights and information. Some White House regulars went for years without riding on the President's plane or serving on a pool that was of any importance. This could only be by design.

Even the wire service reporters were kept in a constant state of agitation about access. They are the ones who, for their own protection and for the protection of the papers and broadcasters who subscribe to their service, bird-dog the President everywhere he goes, unless he manages to slip away without them being informed. At Camp David, the Presidential retreat in northern Maryland, there are no press facilities, yet whenever the President goes there each of the wire services sends a reporter to stay in a nearby motel. The Camp David reporter must telephone back to Washington for any news of the President, but he is close by in the event of an emergency. It is likely that if anything happened to the President at Camp David the stand-by reporters would not be admitted to the grounds. They are there simply to assure the news organizations they serve that they are near the President. Their presence symbolizes the enormous importance Americans have placed in their highest official.

President Nixon, in his desire to get away from the press, frequently would venture into public places with his friend, Charles G. Rebozo, from one of his vacation compounds, with no notification to the press. One weekend at San Clemente, for example, he and Rebozo, accompanied only by secret service agents, went for a long drive over the mountains of Southern California, stopping along the way to mingle with crowds and shake hands. This enraged not only the wire service reporters, who feel a particular weight of responsibility in President watching, but all of the reporters and photographers who would have had to rely on belated second- and third-hand information had there been any kind of newsworthy incident as the President rambled around on his own. Whenever this occurred, which became increasingly often, the reporters would put up a strenuous protest, which was met with bland, oblique explanations by Ziegler or Warren that they were doing the best they could.

There is a day to day dependence of reporters on the press secretary and his staff, yet I do not want to take the plantation analogy too far. The press is an independent entity that was in no sense bound to the White House, even at the height of the Nixon powers. But the necessity for the reporter to obtain news and insights was so compelling that Ziegler could, in many instances, exercise extraordinary control over a reporter's production. In that sense, he was the hated overseer. The system might work like this: President Nixon usually scheduled his most important announcements and speeches for the evening prime television time, which was either on or past the first edition deadline of the Eastern press. This meant one of three things for the *Times:* missing the deadline for a complete edition, rushing the copy into type under enormous production problems, or obtaining an advance copy that would permit careful writing.

Invariably, the press office would say at midday that it was not known whether an advance would be available, but if there was, it probably would be late in the day, or minutes before delivery. An afternoon would be wasted waiting and calling to see when the advance might be ready. Nixon, it was explained, liked to make his revisions up to the last minute. But it seemed more likely, in many instances, that the President and his assistants wanted to keep the contents from leaking in order to build suspense and lead more people to watch the announcement on television. Ziegler knew that news released on deadline was more likely to be printed without analysis. If there ever was a good reason for holding the statement until the last minute, no one in the press believed Ziegler's explanation. It was a little game that was played over and over. We believed that he knew that we knew there was no reason to withhold the advance, and we knew the Nixon White House was not concerned with the needs of the Eastern press, but out of some sense of responsibility we kept on trying.

The press secretary could get a reporter in to see a White House official or he could blackball him and make sure that he saw no one in the inner circle. He could provide him with the information he desired or he could simply cut him off without any help. Ziegler, as an overseer, left much to be desired in the eyes of those dependent on him. He was a different breed from the reporters. A junior public relations executive from Southern California, Ziegler had been propelled into one of the most sensitive offices in the country because he was glib, loyal to the President, hard-working and able to talk forever without saying any more or any less than the President and his assistants wanted. Many of the reporters were older than Ziegler's thirty-four years, having come up in journalism through the usual route of covering the police, city halls, the state houses, politics, Congress—an experience that enhances skepticism of those in public life. They could not understand him, nor could he understand them.

Reinforcing the plantation analogy was the strong feeling among most of the reporters that the Nixon White House was basically corrupt and its press office, day after day, was propagating a lie. Although there was not much evidence early in 1973 to prove it, reporters of sound instinct, such as Helen Thomas of United Press International and Dan Rather of CBS News, believed that White House involvement in the Watergate burglary had been covered up and the cover-up was continuing on a day-to-day basis, exactly as was documented much later. Whether Ziegler was a part of the cover-up or simply had a naïve faith in the President and the institution (in retrospect I believe the latter) did not much matter. The reporter had to deal with a source he did not trust. The difficulty was compounded by the fact that Ziegler maintained a supercilious attitude throughout, except for rare displays of humility, as I will show in a later chapter. Furthermore, reporters can be difficult people. Many turn to journalism out of a sense of insecurity. The White House press, in particular, has more than its share of prima donnas and neurotics.

Under these circumstances, the reactions of reporters varied widely. Some, whose requirements were simply to report what they saw and heard without interpretation, dealt with Ziegler on a rational, businesslike basis. Some were obsequious, as reflected in a June 8 editorial in the Orlando, Florida *Sentinel and Star:* "This clean-cut young man [Ziegler]—whose handsome, deceptive, boyish visage hides a keen mind—is respected by all but a few peevish newspapermen who, fortunately, failed in a try to drive him over Watergate." Actually, a large majority of the White House press was peevish, and more. If they gave Ziegler the benefit of the doubt and assumed that he was not part of the cover-up, they had to conclude that he did not display the quality that Robert J. McCloskey, the former State Department spokesman who was highly regarded by reporters, said was essential to the role of spokesman: "the discrimination to detect, even from a distance, the barest scent of the false." This could be even more maddening to reporters than intentional deception. Thus there was, in the President's press entourage, an abundance of frustration and neurosis not always suppressed. For my own purposes, I felt it was best for me to have as little as possible to do with Ziegler, despite the risk of lack of access that seemed important at the time.

5
A MIRROR IMAGE

Like the passing of the Dark Ages, it is difficult to set a precise time when the Nixon regime, with all of its enormous powers, first started to unravel. Undoubtedly, it was at some point during the spring of 1973, following a rash of news stories pointing to White House involvement in the burglary and bugging of Democratic headquarters in the Watergate complex the previous June 17. The news stories stemmed in part from the decision of James McCord, one of the Watergate burglars, to implicate White House officials, a decision that was made after Judge John J. Sirica threatened long prison terms for the guilty. Investigative reporters, working behind the scenes with prosecutors and others, kept up a steady stream of new disclosures that went higher and higher into the White House hierarchy. The job for the White House reporter became primarily to report what was happening in the administration as a result of the disclosures and to interpret what it all meant.

What the President was doing about policies and about governing the country—which had long been of primary concern—became secondary to Nixon's strange defense of his Presidency and a series of surrealistic occurrences that seem now to have even more of an illogical quality when viewed against the subsequent proof from the White House tapes: that the President and his top assistants, even as the disclosures were unfolding in March and April 1973, were conspiring to cover up White House involvement in the Watergate case and were recording it all, never knowing that the recordings would later be used to drive the President from office and convict his assistants of felonies.

There was the April 30 television appearance in which the President, after announcing the resignations of H. R. Haldeman, John D. Ehrlichman, and Attorney General Richard G. Kleindienst and the dismissal of John Dean, the White House lawyer who was beginning to talk to prosecutors, accepted the responsibility, but not the blame, for Watergate and said in pious tones, "There can be no whitewash at the White House." There was Ron Ziegler, still cocky and authoritative, saying a few days later, "Any reference or suggestion made by anyone that the President would have proceeded in any other way than to provide information for the court is completely unfounded." There was the Easter vacation in Key Biscayne where the President went to church and heard the Reverend John A. Huffman, Jr. talk about sin and redemption and the need to break away from crooked friends; and on the same day Nixon called John Dean, who was in the process of implicating the President in Watergate, and in wishing him a happy Easter assured him, "You are still my counsel." "A stroking call," Dean later called it.

There was the 4,000-word statement of May 22, in which Nixon admitted to some White House efforts to conceal some aspects of the Watergate case but said those actions stemmed from his legitimate interest in protecting national security; then two days later he went before 610 cheering former prisoners of war and lashed out at those who threaten the secrecy of national security matters, an overt attempt to shift the focus of public attention from the Watergate case to the broad issue of national defense. There was the repeated exercise of "executive privilege" in which the President refused to turn over the documents to Congress and prosecutors on the grounds that doing so would weaken the office of the President for himself and his successors.

And so it was to continue for more than a year, the President cutting his losses as close as possible while moving from one defense strategy to the other. In the process, his administration became progressively weaker as the tight control he had held on the governmental bureaucracy and on Congress relaxed. He was forced to reorganize the executive branch, moving his officials from one post to another, yet seldom bringing in new talent because of the difficulty of recruiting against the stigma of Watergate. Authority flowed from the White House back to the bureaucracy and Congress reasserted its prerogatives, moving against Presidential war powers and spending authority.

Yet one thing that never changed was the Nixon public relations apparatus. In mid-1973, there was considerable informed opinion that Mr. Nixon could put Watergate behind him by appearing before one or more congressional committees to answer questions and display his cooperation, by installing a new press secretary who would better understand the role of the press and who could dispell some of the poisonous atmosphere in the press room, by opening himself to the press in the way previous Presidents had done, and by being a little more modest in his living style. It was not known at the time, of course, of the existence of the tapes or the depth of Presidential involvement. Nevertheless, there is no doubt that he could have done himself a considerable amount of good by taking those steps as an act necessary for survival. He never did, though, for reasons to be discussed in a later chapter. He rejected the recommendation of at least two top aides—Melvin R. Laird and John B. Connally—to move Ziegler out of the press office, saying at one point, "They (the press) will not get that pound of flesh." Nor could he, according to several accounts, bring himself to see journalists for interviews, background sessions, or simply social gatherings—a public relations device that could have dispelled the dark suspicions festering in the news rooms. In the White House press corps, contrary to the popular saying, nothing breeds contempt like unfamiliarity with the President.

As the Watergate disclosures increased, so did criticism of the President for his lavish mode of living. But rather than curtail his travel and live more economically, Nixon did the opposite. He traveled more than he had before, which was often, calling attention to the enormous public expense involved, much of it, as it turned out, illegally or improperly acquired. Almost every weekend he either went to Camp David, a government-owned hideaway and amusement park in the Cotoctin Mountains, or to Key Biscayne, where he had a home on the bay. From Key Biscayne, Nixon frequently went by helicopter to the home of a friend, Robert H. Abplanalp on Grand Cay in the Bahamas. Three or four times a year he would go to his home in San Clemente for two to three weeks.

The excesses of the Nixon expenditures have been amply documented elsewhere. The point here is to show that his constant travels drew attention to such questionable self-indulgences as the extraordinary number of private offices he maintained. Because the Oval Office at the White House was too formal, Nixon had a hideaway office in the Executive Office Building and he equipped the Lincoln Room, in the Presidential apartment, as another office. At Camp David he had the office other Presidents had used and he had another one installed in a nearby lodge. He had an office at his home in Key Biscayne and another at the Abplanalp home on Grand Cay. In San Clemente, his official office was in the complex of government buildings on Coast Guard land bordering the Pacific—the Western White House, as the Nixon people called it—and he had another hideaway office on the second floor of the Spanish-style Nixon mansion adjacent to the Coast Guard property—nine in all, each equipped with the sophisticated communications facilities required for the nation's chief executive.

A Presidential trip to anywhere is an impressive sight. On my first trip to Key Biscayne, I could hardly believe so much movement and expense could go into one weekend vacation. Before the President arrived, I was told, fleets of Air Force jets swept over Cuba and the broad expanse of water around Miami to make sure no alien enemy was organizing an assault. When the chartered press plane landed at Homestead Air Force Base, a fleet of five Air Force helicopters were waiting. Scores of advance men, technicians, and servants had been at work making ready for the traveling White House. The blue and silver Presidential jet—a Boeing 707 known as Air Force One, but which the Nixon White House, in its fascination with public relations, named *The Spirit of '76*—arrived gleaming and majestic as usual. Even the inside of the jet cowling had the appearance of newly minted metal, finely honed. Following Air Force One was another jet just like it, carrying personnel and odds and ends.

Out of Air Force One poured the President and his entourage—members of the White House staff, their wives and children, functionaries of various kinds and the press pool—a body of about forty people on this particular trip. They piled into the helicopters and took off for Key Biscayne. Meantime, platoons of Air Force men in white raced with scores of pieces of luggage and equipment to other helicopters, which took off minutes after the President and his party. The luggage could have been carried by truck to the Presidential compound in two hours, but by air the luggage could be delivered in fifteen minutes. Cost to the public mattered to no one. That is the way things are done in the White House.

The long days in the sun at Key Biscayne may have raised the President's spirits but they could only have exacerbated his Watergate troubles. If Nixon was isolated and depicted as a reclusive, pouting President in Washington, he was more so in Florida, for there the curtain completely went down between the President and reporters, and the suspicions of reporters transported from Washington grew. The Presidential compound on Key Biscayne was off limits to reporters. The bulk of them were housed in the Four Ambassadors Hotel in Miami, five miles across the Causeway. At the Four Ambassadors, the press room was set up in a flimsy building that had been a model for condominiums, and there the reporters found only the skimpiest and unreliable contact with the Presidential party.

Before the Watergate disclosures, I was told, the press occasionally would be permitted in the Presidential compound and, in fact, as late as one Sunday morning in January 1973, when Nixon and Kissinger were preparing for the Paris peace accords, we were ushered in to watch, from behind a rope, the officials talking on the lawn. But as the Watergate disclosures came, even the briefings in the ramshackle press room grew infrequent. And the President's aides were increasingly disinclined to return telephone calls, and when they did they were usually not responsive to what the reporter wanted to know.

Ron Ziegler and Alexander M. Haig, Jr., the army general who had replaced Haldeman as chief of staff, would show up from time to time at the tennis courts of the Royal Biscayne Hotel, where the reporters who played the game worked off their frustrations, but they rarely conveyed any information of importance. There were postings in the press room of the President's activities from time to time, but this did not diminish the fear a number of us expressed openly: that the Presidency, as an institution that had always been reported with some degree of access, was slipping away from our view. I would not have been surprised if Nixon, on his frequent vacations, had simply abolished the pretense of the press room and the formalized contact between press and the White House. For through most of 1973, I believe that nearly everyone in the Nixon White House thought that the President was very much in control of events and would prevail in the end. There was deeper concern than Nixon and his associates displayed publicly at the time. The tape recordings would later disclose their fears and uncertainties. I learned long after Nixon left office that one of the secretaries in the press office was kept up all night of Easter eve 1973 transcribing by telephone the Watergate stories from the *Times* and the *Washington Post* just so the President and his assistants, who were affecting a public show of little concern about the scandals, would know what was printed a few hours before the Sunday delivery of those papers. But a false sense of security was one of the earmarks of the Nixon White House almost until the end.

As information became harder to come by through traditional means, it became necessary to sharpen one's perceptions. That was what made the reporting of John Osborne in the *New Republic* so outstanding during this period. If none of the public statements and actions of the President and his assistants made sense, as frequently was the case, Osborne would examine a situation from several perspectives, from above, from below, from all sides, and put together a conclusion of sound insight. To be at all right, I felt I had to know the basic premises of the President's attitudes towards the troubles besetting him. Over a period of time I learned that Ziegler was almost a mirror reflection of what was on the President's mind, not in what he said the President was thinking, but what Ziegler said on his own in his ramblings about the Watergate situation. Without becoming entangled with Ziegler and his games, I began to listen to him more closely for small clues, especially after he was made a daily confidant to the President without giving up his responsibilities for running the public relations apparatus.

In late August 1973, President Nixon was in San Clemente for the second time that summer. The Senate Watergate Committee hearings had ended, Nixon had held his first press conference in five months to answer the charges of John Dean, his former counsel, that he was part of the cover-up, and relations between the press and the White House were becoming more and more embittered. It was not only Watergate. A dozen areas of possible wrong-doing were being probed daily by the press and the prosecutors. One was the question of how Nixon bought his San Clemente estate. Why did the President conceal for three months the fact that his good friend, C. G. Rebozo, teamed with Robert Abplanalp to relieve the President of financial pressures by buying part of the land on the estate? How could a President who had little independent wealth expect to pay a note of $226,000—more than his yearly salary of $200,000 —on his San Clemente and Key Biscayne homes that would be due within a year? These questions had gone on in the daily press briefings for weeks, and to stem the criticism, Nixon hired a New York auditing firm, Coopers & Lybrand, to conduct an audit of the complicated transactions.

On August 27, Nixon released the audit report in a bitter-end effort to end the controversy "once and for all," as his spokesmen put it. It was a lengthy, complex document, as almost everything issued by Nixon on controversial issues tended to be. And, as could be expected, it was made available at midday, close to deadline for the Eastern papers and the television networks. There was not much time for study and checking, as Ziegler and his assistants knew quite well.

It was one of those occasions when I was glad to be working for the *Times*, which has specialists on almost everything. Wallace Turner, chief of the San Francisco bureau and one of the best investigative reporters in the country, came down to write the story and I did what I could to help him. When the President was in San Clemente, the press was quartered at the Surf & Sand Motel at Laguna Beach, about fifteen miles north of the Presidential compound. There was a press room at one end of the motel's Polynesian restaurant and another at the San Clemente Inn, about a mile from the Nixon home. The audit report was released in Laguna Beach.

Rather than work in the confusion of the press room, Wally and I retired to his room in the motel. Despite the volume of the document, Wally soon discovered that it did not answer all the questions. One of the routine checks we made was a call to the *Times'* research department in New York for any background information on Coopers & Lybrand. In a few moments one of the researchers called back and told me that two former officials of the auditing firm were fined for mail fraud in 1968 and had been given pardons by President Nixon in December 1972. By any standard of journalism this fact belonged in the story. More sensational papers would have made a big thing of it, especially in view of the fact that it was not known to anyone else covering the story. Wally, in his usual exercise of restraint, inserted it a few paragraphs down in his story, which he was then filing on deadline.

The *Times* has a fairness rule which requires reporters to inform the person involved of any derogatory information about to be published about him in order to give him an opportunity to respond, to refute, or explain the allegation or fact. Of course, it was not possible to call the President. I called the press office, as we had done rather routinely over the weeks and months as the Watergate disclosures surfaced in the newspapers. I gave the information to Diane Sawyer, a bright and attractive young assistant to Ziegler. In a few minutes she called back to say Ziegler wanted to see me in his office. The tone of her voice indicated something was wrong. My inclination was to reply that if Mr. Ziegler wanted to see me he could come to the room, but I checked this impulse by reminding myself my purpose was to gather and relay information, not to serve my ego.

The Surf & Sand Motel is a tower built on the Pacific with every room having an ocean view. Wally's room was on a corner looking down the beach toward San Clemente. It was then mid-afternoon and the scene, as I descended two flights of outside stairs, was one of incredible beauty. The blue and white of the surf breaking against sand and enormous rocks, gave way to hills of delicate browns, greens, and yellows broken by low rectangular houses of many colors anchored on the cliffs. I wondered, as I had many times in the past, what effect such idyllic settings, to which Nixon seemed constantly retreating, and which were so far removed from the sweat pits and teeming cities where so many Americans spent their lives, had on Presidential decision-making.

It all seemed so strange. Yet here, too, was a little war, between the press, which was determined to expose the full extent of official corruption, and the Presidency, which was equally determined that the inquiry be broken off and the President be permitted to return to what he considered his rightful role of bringing about a new world order.

Diane Sawyer met me in the press office, a large room off the elevators where Ziegler's staff worked with their telephones, typewriters and mimeograph machines. She was cordial, as usual, but looked pale and drained. When the President was in San Clemente, she had to arise at 4 A.M. daily, which was 7 A.M. in Washington, to pull together information of various kinds, and her duties usually kept her until late at night. Ziegler drove his staff hard, and one of the wonders of the Nixon Presidency was that throughout the entire Watergate period no one resigned, neither from overwork nor from inability to serve the Nixon White House. There was never any doubt that their loyalty was to Ziegler and to Nixon and, with one or two exceptions, they shared the view that the press was conducting a vendetta against their boss. Yet they maintained friendly relations with reporters. Not so Ziegler.

I was told that Ziegler was waiting for me in his private office. He was in a rage. He began by saying that everyone on *The New York Times,* with one or two possible exceptions, had lost all sense of fair play. Coopers & Lybrand was a highly regarded firm, he said, which had been chosen, not by the President, but by H. Chapman Rose of Cleveland and Kenneth W. Gemmill of Philadelphia, two respected tax lawyers who had volunteered to help Nixon with his financial matters. The two fined auditors, he explained, had long since left the firm and it never occurred to anyone involved that the pardons would make any difference.

What he wanted me to do, it became clear as he raged on, was not simply to print his explanation, which we duly did, but to delete any reference to the pardons. His argument was that this item was not newsworthy, that as soon as our story appeared on the streets in New York, this fact would be picked up and played prominently by the wire services and broadcast stations, and the whole purpose of the audit—to finally clear the President of wrongdoing in the purchase of the San Clemente estate—would be overshadowed. As he talked his anger grew. He became abusive of the *Times,* saying at one point that the paper had lost all sense of fairness. I made a hasty retreat, explaining we were on deadline and I would see what Wally wanted to do, because it was his story.

Wally, to his credit, was not impressed by Ziegler or his anger. As one who had to work on the plantation, I was more upset than I should have been. But there was never any thought that we would back down. In a few minutes, Ziegler called me back to his office. I told him that we were running the information, along with his explanation—anger deleted; we would be happy to run any statement Coopers & Lybrand wanted to make; and that the matter of the pardon was in the body of the story, not the lead. He was angrier than before. I had had long experience with angry news sources, from sheriffs, governors, and prosecutors in the South during the civil rights days, to Washington officials, and I had learned not to respond in kind but to let them talk, sometime to the extent of seeming phlegmatic. Perhaps this was rationalization for my inclination to avoid a fight, but I do not ever remember anger deterring my course of reporting.

Ziegler was not impressed by my statements that it was the collective wisdom of many on the *Times* that the pardon was a proper element of the story that should be reported in perspective. There was no communication between us. We were from different worlds and we might as well have spoken different languages. He was then a young man who for five years had been at the center of power. Although he did not say so, it was clear to me that he viewed himself as in a position of authority and felt a burden to act on that authority.

As he talked it became obvious that his anger was directed not so much at the *Times,* as at what he considered a higher and more important enemy of the President—the office of the special prosecutor, then headed by Archibald Cox. The people in that office were liberal Democrats of the anti-Nixon, pro-Kennedy mold engaged in a battle to the death with the Nixon White House. Ziegler thought someone in Cox's office had given the *Times* the information about the pardon, and I could not persuade him otherwise, even though I was under no obligation to tell him where the information came from. How did I know, he asked, that the information did not come from the prosecutors? It came from our information division in New York, I replied, as a matter of a routine check. Could I prove that?

I did not know where the information about the Nixon pardon originated, but I was certain the *Times'* librarians were not in touch with the special prosecutor's office. By the time I pulled myself away from Ziegler that evening it was too late in New York to check. The next morning I called and learned that the story of the pardons had appeared on the front page of the *Times* at the time they were made, and our researcher simply pulled it from the files in response to my inquiry. Minutes later Ziegler was on the telephone wanting to know what I had found. When I told him, he was at last convinced, and he was very cordial.

I did not know whether Ziegler had been talking to the President after his explosion of the day before. But it did not matter. Ziegler's mind was by then Nixon's mind, and I knew that the President did not consider the investigations against him legitimate pursuits, but purely political efforts to drive him from office. This belief, however jaundiced and unrealistic, was central to almost everything Nixon did until he was forced to resign. And it ran so deep and so strong it suggested a mind gone awry. It was helpful to me to know this with certainty at that time. Although I never told him, I was almost grateful to Ziegler for his explosion.

At the end of the California stay, there was a surprise. For the first time in the eight months that I had been covering the White House, I was assigned to the Air Force One pool. Ziegler always pays his debts, someone said. A few days later, I found on my desk in the White House press room, a fourteen by eleven-inch card bearing the Presidential seal, a full-color picture of Air Force One, and these words:

FLIGHT CERTIFICATE

This is to certify that

John Herbers

has flown in Air Force One as a guest of Richard Nixon,
President of the United States of America
Presented this 31st day of August 1973

(Signed) Ralph Albetarge
(the pilot)

No matter that the *Times* had paid more than first-class fare for me to be Richard Nixon's "guest." At last I was a full-fledged White House correspondent.

6
NO THANK YOU, MR. PRESIDENT

In July and August at San Clemente, day usually begins with fog shrouding the beaches and brown hills. But well before noon the sun has burnt away the vapor, the sparkle of green palms and blue Pacific is visible for miles and the air is clean and cool. It was that kind of day on August 22, 1973, when at 11:30 A.M., some fifty reporters were seated on folding chairs on the lawn of the Western White House for the first Presidential press conference in five months. Across the nation, millions of television sets were turned on in anticipation of hearing and seeing Nixon submit to his first questioning of the Watergate charges that had been so dramatically presented, from May 17 until August 7, by Senator Sam Ervin's Senate Watergate Committee.

It had been a long time since I had felt such tension—like the stress just before entering combat, some veterans later noted—and it was particularly acute for me because I was new as a participant in that unique institution called the Presidential news conference. I had been a reporter for twenty-four years and every fiber in my being told me that I did not belong there. I did not mind going on television and asking a question and being seen by relatives and old friends. I was as vain as the rest. But by training and experience, I was convinced the role of the reporter should be one of unobtrusive observer. In the Presidential press conference, the reporter, whether he wishes it or not, is part of the story, and how can a reporter report honestly about himself? This was true even before Richard Nixon set up the press as a straw man to be accused and bayoneted.

The Presidential news conference had long been more show business and a device for the President to promote himself than a session of inquiry to uncover news. Television has served a valuable purpose in covering the Presidency. It puts the President closer to the people, who can then observe him for themselves. Lyndon Johnson could not hide his deviousness from the public he sought to persuade by his frequent appearances. Television freed the print reporter from much of the drudgery of simply writing what the President said, and permitted him to search for another dimension of the story. There is no longer the mindless stampede from the news conference to the telephone, because by the time the conference is over, the news already is on the teletype machines and in newsrooms across the country.

As a televised spectacular, however, the conference is seriously flawed. In the informal news conferences that mayors, governors, congressmen, and other officials hold, daily a reporter can develop not only the hard news but the insights and feel for the official that is important to the interpretive copy he writes. The Presidential press conference is staged and plastic. Why should a President, who is performing his job on a day to day basis, have to be so elaborately briefed and coached for thirty minutes of questioning? Scores of people are put to work long before the event anticipating questions and suggesting answers. It is an institutionalized system that grew, I believe, out of the cult of the Presidency which holds that the President is no mere mortal who might answer, "I don't know much about that subject at this stage. I will try to provide answers later." As it is, we do not know whether the answers he gives are his or those of some unnamed assistant who told him what to say. We do not have much sense of his own grasp of the government, or of his style, or substance.

Both the President and his questioners are caught up in drama. For comic relief he can call on a reporter known for outlandish questions. He can determine the course of the conference by opening it with a provocative statement on a particular subject that cries out for further explanation and thus draws a number of questions in that area. He can select hard questions or soft questions by choosing the appropriate reporters, the most predictable of people. He can filibuster and engage in demagoguery.

Reporters become actors on a stage. They scream for recognition. Once recognized, they frequently deliver an oration before coming to the question. Like a politician on a soap box, they say in one hundred words what could be said in ten. Or they pose a question designed more to embarrass the President than to get an answer that will make news. The initial purpose of the news conference, to provide disclosures and information for use in news stories, is forgotten in the theatrics of it all.

President Nixon succeeded in making every negative aspect of the press conference worse than before, and he got considerable help from the press. He held conferences so infrequently that there was no way the subjects to which he was obligated to address himself could be covered in the short time allotted. This led to the incongruous effect of burning questions going unasked or unsatisfactory answers that were never followed up. When he chose to depict the press as an enemy unfairly attacking him, he called on reporters sure to ask the most outrageous questions. He gave long, convoluted answers to unimportant questions, thus limiting the scope of the conference. He distorted facts just enough so that the correct version never caught up with his televised account. After each press conference, much of the daily press briefings was taken up correcting Nixon misstatements.

The San Clemente conference set the tone for subsequent ones as Nixon fought to retain his office. When Nixon appeared, he seemed as nervous as the reporters. A blue velvet curtain had been set up as a backdrop—the obsession with appearances would continue to the end—and Nixon, his face a ruddy tan, took his place at the microphones and faced into the sun. Wishing to divert as much attention as possible to his direction of foreign affairs, Nixon began with a long announcement that he was appointing Kissinger, his foreign policy adviser, as secretary of state, to replace William P. Rogers. Virtually every question, however, concerned Watergate or related matters, a development that enraged Nixon. Yet this was to be expected, because his television appearance of August 15, in which he sought to lay the Watergate charges to rest, left a host of unanswered questions.

Because of the assignment of seats to the news organizations that regularly cover the President, I was seated in the second row. When he recognized me for a question, I stood rather nervously and asked, "Mr. President, do you still consider Haldeman and Ehrlichman two of the finest public servants you have ever known?" He had so described them in announcing their resignations on April 30. "I certainly do," he replied, and when his eyes met mine, I thought I detected a disturbing mixture of intense pain and anger. It had been a long time since I described him as the nicest man in North Dakota, and I do not know to this day whether he remembered me.

In the midst of the fifty-minute session, Nixon broke in to say, "Just a moment. We have had thirty minutes of this press conference. I have yet to have, for example, one question on the business of the people, which shows you how we are consumed with this. I am not criticizing members of the press because you naturally are interested in this issue [Watergate], but let me tell you, years from now people are going to perhaps be interested in what happened in terms of the efforts of the United States to build a structure of peace in the world."

Then he recognized James Deakin of the *St. Louis Post-Dispatch*, who had been covering the White House since Eisenhower and the reporter who was most likely to ask the most biting Watergate question of all. Deakin, fulfilling expectations, asked if the President should not be the object of impeachment proceedings, which at that time was generally considered to be an impertinent idea. Then, with Dan Rather of CBS News, the exchange was as follows:

RATHER: Mr. President, I want to state this question with due respect to your office, but also as directly as possible.
THE PRESIDENT: That would be unusual. [Laughter]
RATHER: I would like to think not. It concerns . . .
THE PRESIDENT: [with irony] You are always respectful, Mr. Rather. You know that.

This baiting of the press was to increase in subsequent conferences and some reporters, especially those in broadcasting, fell into his trap, I thought, by arguing back. In retrospect, it seems that public opinion may have been on the side of the press, but at the time there was a considerable body of opinion which held with Nixon that the media was unfairly attacking the President and that he was right to accuse the media of carrying on a vendetta. The questions and statements that seemed to bait the President only increased this feeling and damaged the integrity of all White House reporting. It was good show business, it was raw conflict, the stuff that drama is made of, and we all were guilty of squeezing that drama for all it was worth. The old-fashioned idea that the news conference was intended to produce information and insight seemed to have been forgotten. But the attempts to needle the conflict for effect was never good journalism, neither for television nor for newspapers.

As a means of arriving at the truth, the remaining Nixon news conferences, which continued to be infrequent, were worth little more than the sit-down television presentations in which the President addressed the nation. The influences of show biz took almost total control. At one conference in the East Room of the White House, the shouting of reporters for recognition was the most notable occurrence. The conferences were to improve remarkably when Gerald Ford, a man who offered a marked contrast to his precedessor in character and style, took office, although the basic flaws remained, as will be pointed out in a later chapter. It was under Nixon, however, that the press conference was needed most, and it was under Nixon that its weaknesses were most apparent and it served its purposes less than at any time in the past. And the reason was not just in the peculiar circumstances of the final months of the Nixon Presidency. The reason also was in what past Presidents and the media had made of it since the days when Franklin D. Roosevelt or Harry S. Truman would have reporters into the office once or twice a week to ask the questions that were on their minds.

The spontaneity had long gone out of the Presidential press conference, and it was not just because of television. It had become encrusted and sterile in the process of the overaggrandizement of the office, the building of a large and structured White House staff, and the general acquiescence to the idea that the Presidency could and should shape public opinion far beyond the ability of the other institutions to do so. The press conference was and is the President's, not the public's, device. Despite the fact that Nixon frightened a lot of people by his behavior, I do not believe the press conferences helped much in bringing about his resignation. On the contrary, it seemed that they enabled him to hold on longer.

7
CHASING
IMPRESSIONS

A reporter for a newspaper does not ordinarily receive much mail from readers. If newspaper subscribers have something to say they usually address it to the "Letters to the Editor" column, of which the *Times* receives an enormous volume daily. When Nixon's Watergate troubles became the center of national attention, however, I began receiving far more letters than I could answer. Some were complimentary or offered suggestions. A woman from Greensboro, North Carolina, wanted me to find out how many people around the country who cheered Nixon in his public appearances were being paid to do so. From Staten Island, New York, a reader wrote, "I recently read that Rose Mary Woods, 'Tricky's secretary, pays $1,400 per month (plus expenses) for an apartment at Watergate. Is this woman independently wealthy? Or are we poor, exploited, middle- and lower-income taxpayers paying for this luxury. Will you please investigate and let your reading public know the score on the above?" [Precisely how much Miss Woods spent for her apartment could not be learned by this reporter. She had long since quit talking to the press about personal matters. However, such rentals were not unusual for the Watergate complex, and Miss Woods earned more than $40,000 a year with only herself to support.] A man from Detroit wrote, "I have long suspected that part of President Nixon's political philosophy was Machiavellian in its classical sense. . . . Lately I have even suspected the possibility that President Nixon may have been influenced by the late nineteenth-century German philosopher, Friedrich Nietzsche." And so on.

The great majority of the letters, however, were hostile to my reporting and that of the media generally. Most of this was not what we call "nut mail," that is, diatribes from unstable people who regularly write to newspapers and reporters, especially those in Washington, describing the wrongs of the world and who is to blame. The majority of letters seemed to be from stable Americans, some well-educated, who were deeply disturbed that the press was tearing up the foundations of United States democracy by its attacks, even its critical analyses, on the President. I thought the letters came from that hard core 25 percent who expressed their support of the President in the public opinion polls month after month, no matter what the disclosures of wrongdoing.

"Aren't you ashamed when you read this article you have written?" wrote a woman from New Hope, Pennsylvania, who enclosed a news analysis I had done on President Nixon as a recluse and his fights with the press. "Everything is written with the effort to make the President look bad."

A woman in Kansas City, enclosing the same analysis from the *Kansas City Times,* was less restrained: "If you have wives and children, how very proud they must be of the notches in your guns and the scalps in your tepees of the lives you have wrecked. You dog every footstep of President Nixon, spying and searching for a minor incident to pump up into a printed lie. You allow him no privacy in his home or with his family, and try your very best to involve his personal friends in false positions."

A man in Clearwater, Florida, wrote, "Some extremists are doing all they can to tear down Mr. Nixon, the government and, of course, this wonderful country. . . . I don't want to be critical; I prefer to be constructive. Why don't you go hear Dr. Norman Vincent Peale and learn about 'Positive Thinking.' And read his books. You must have some desirable qualifications! Build on them! Disparaging our PRESIDENT is a dubious occupation."

A man, whose address I have lost, wrote by pencil on lined paper, "The nation and world are throbbing with fast-moving events while you and other petty vendors are getting in the gutter looking for peanuts a monkey dropped. . . . President Nixon, faults and all, has done more for this nation than Kennedy and Johnson. De Gaulle saved France and history may say Nixon saved America."

From Enfield, North Carolina, a man wrote, "Mr. Nixon has made us the best President we have *ever* had in my day and I will be ninety-one years old February 10, 1974. He stopped the war started by Kennedy and kept going by Johnson, brought thousands of our soldier boys home from the firing line and prison, and you dare to speak disrespectible [*sic*] about such a man."

"Look around, Mr. Herbers," wrote a woman from Muncy, Pennsylvania, "The world is going to smash while the NYT engages in murdering the President and depriving free people of our strength and our stability." From Hazard, Kentucky, a woman wrote, "Please cease using the President as a whipping post. . . . For several years it has been obvious to thinking people that the news media must use self-discipline."

It was a little unsettling to get these letters day after day. Who were these people? Obviously they were on the right politically. They did not seem to be an organized writing bloc. They could not be dismissed as cranks, although some of them obviously fit that category. When I was working in the South I had noticed that the ideological right, which held up the American creed of justice for all, despite its frequent violation, sometimes subscribed to the liberal line a generation or two after its inception. Harry Truman is now the hero of Dixiecrats who hated him in 1948. The letter writers defended Nixon because, in their minds, he represented what they believed in. But it was more than that. They had somewhere along the way accepted the concept for a super Presidency—which for years had been popular on the left—even though their spiritual ancestors had feared centralized government. To them it was sacrilege for anyone to malign the President, especially one who supported their concept of world order and moral discipline at home. Like that of a king, his personal behavior, they insisted, was beside the point. It never occurred to them to look to Congress, the bulwark of conservative government in the past, or to a dispersal of authority among other government institutions, for a constitutional way out.

The intensity of the pro-Nixon feeling among this segment of the electorate had not escaped the notice of the President and his assistants. Nixon would take time from a busy day to meet with grass-roots leaders of the movement. A joke among reporters was that the surest way to get an appointment with the President of the United States was to circulate a petition or take out a newspaper advertisement in Nixon's behalf. In many communities, the movement was organized by housewives out of their kitchens. One day, Mrs. Leslie Dutton of Malibu, California, stood before the President in the Oval Office and unrolled a long scroll containing pro-Nixon signatures. "These coupons come from the west side of Los Angeles," she said. "It's a great country," the President replied. "It's Nixon country," she said.

The job of caring for this constituency, which became of increasing importance to the President, fell to Bruce Herschensohn, deputy special assistant to the President. Of all the people in the Nixon White House I could not understand, Herschensohn perhaps led the list. He was friendly and creative; he had been a television producer who had done some fine work for the United States Information Agency. He had served under Lyndon Johnson and had stayed on after the change of administrations to become one of Richard Nixon's most partisan admirers.

Even more than the grass-roots, pro-Nixon constituency, Herschensohn was obsessed by what he termed unfair media coverage, especially by television. He appeared on talk and panel shows espousing that view. I thought the frequency with which he was invited damaged his argument. But in any event, he was more open and cooperative and easier to talk to than any of the other Nixon aides. He let me see stacks of White House mail for a story I was preparing on the Nixon people. These letters were in the same vein as those I had received. "Americans certainly should come to realize," wrote a man from Atlantic City, New Jersey, "that more than the man Richard Nixon is at stake. The office of the Presidency is hanging on the ledge. Is Mr. Nixon to be judged as a politician or as a statesman and a President?"

The Nixon defense, of course, was organized around that concept, that the Presidency, not the man, was under attack. The chief leader of the grass-roots movement was Rabbi Baruch Korff who was chairman of the National Citizens Committee for Fairness to the Presidency. Some of my colleagues thought he was a cheap opportunist out to make a fast buck and get publicity. After talking to him at length in his cluttered, second-floor office on Connecticut Avenue, I did not agree with so simple an assessment. He was something of an actor. He seemed to enjoy describing how he had suffered three heart attacks and every moment he spent working for the President put him closer to his grave, all the while he appeared to be thriving in the limelight. But I had to admire what he had done. He had started a newspaper advertising campaign in behalf of Nixon from a shoestring budget and had collected several hundred thousand dollars in the process. He was an immigrant from the Ukraine who developed a deep faith in the American system. I thought he had a naïve understanding of the system but that he sincerely believed it was being damaged by the impeachment movement, however constitutional it was.

Because the grass-roots movement of which Rabbi Korff was a part seemed to be an important factor in the Nixon defense, I wrote a two-column story describing it. And because of the acute sensitivity to media bias in the movement, I took special pains to be fair, quoting participants at length and treating the movement as a legitimate, important force. The story ran on page one, under a two-column head, exactly as I wrote it. Bruce Herschensohn thanked me for it. When I asked Rabbi Korff for comment, out of an intense curiosity to learn what people like him consider fair, he said, "It could have been better. But I don't think it was your fault. I think you were circumcised by your editors." This was typical, I thought, of the way the harshest critics of the press see a conspiracy in every development. It was possible for them to conceive of a reporter as honest and fair, but the editors, those in control of the paper, were to them a necessary part of the conspiracy that required distortion in order to shape the news to a liberal bias. It was my own experience that editors, by and large, are more conservative than reporters. In any event, most of my critics gave me, as a reporter, sufficient credit for being part of the conspiracy. One of the Korff faithful, a man in New Rochelle, New York, wrote, "It was good of you to take notice of our existence in your column today. However, I would like to make one small correction to your intriguing little piece—we do not have 'distrust' for the media, the proper noun is 'disgust'. Other than that it was not a bad show on your part, with no more than the usual number of errors."

This experience underscored for me the depth of antimedia feeling in large segments of the American population. The Watergate era only gave it another means of bubbling to the surface, as Spiro Agnew had done in the first Nixon term when he berated print and broadcast journalism for bias. As far as the White House is concerned, both the rise of modern communications and the aggrandizement of the Presidency have contributed to the honest conviction on the part of many people that most of the media acts out of bias in conveying information. The modern White House has the means of overwhelming the public with its point of view, through its command of television, its ability to overshadow other institutions that might offer another point of view, and its control over the entire executive branch, which makes up no small part of the forces of power in the United States. It is when the media tries to interpret developments in a way that is counter to the White House view that the charges of bias arise.

The Nixon White House wanted nothing less than an uncritical conveying of its official line. Previous administrations had desired the same, but never with the intensity that the Nixon people showed. They were incensed, and said so, on reading and hearing day after day the media's interpretation, rather than the official one, of what was taking place. Beyond that, there were impressions and perceptions I began to form that made more of an impact on me than overt occurrences. For example, during the summit meetings that Nixon held with Soviet leader Leonid I. Brezhnev in 1973 and 1974, there was a rapport among some of the American and Russian officials that to me was unsettling. I expect American officials to respect and promote democratic processes. I expect Soviet officials to pursue authoritarian ways, because that is the way their government works. While nothing was ever said to confirm it, I felt the Nixon officials envied the control exercised by the Soviets. Ron Ziegler and Leonid M. Zamyatin, general director of TASS, the Soviet news agency, seemed to get on famously, which was all right. What was disturbing was that in their joint briefings, Ziegler and Zamyatin seemed to give similar answers in the same spirit of we-the-government-know-best, which most Americans find distasteful. At a briefing in San Clemente in 1973, for example, the two officials sat side by side and were so disdainfully vague in their answers to questions that only their accents distinguished the American from the Russian.

Again, through Ziegler, I felt I was looking into Nixon's mind, and there was a resentment of the democratic processes there, deep-seated and basic, that I had never detected in any of the American political leaders I had covered over the years. All of this was totally impressionistic, but it was more convincing to me than what was said or the criminal evidence that was accumulating in the Congress and the special prosecutor's office. Words at the White House no longer had any meaning.

In briefing after briefing, Ziegler and Gerald Warren had explained away the most blatant contradictions as a matter of semantics. If a White House official such as Melvin R. Laird or Anne Armstrong, both Presidential counselors, conceded that Watergate was hampering the administration or hurting the party, the President's spokesmen, touting the official line that the government was functioning unhampered and the party potential was unscathed, would concede no disagreement. It was just a matter of interpretation, they said.

I did not realize how my approach to reporting had changed until some event such as a summit meeting would occur and the State Department reporters would show up. They would scurry around, buttonholing officials in search of evidence of the extent of the détente that the Americans and Soviets were pursuing. This was reporting as I had known it over the years, and it was still important to do. But I was into something different. The story for the White House regulars was the condition of Nixon and his administration and what he was doing for survival. More important than what the Nixon White House was *doing* in its official capacity was what it *was*. On this story, no one on the inside who I knew could be believed. While the State Department reporters sought bits and pieces of foreign policy, I sought bits and pieces of impressions. The people who wrote me those disturbing letters no doubt would have wanted me to report the official line—which, of course, I continued to do—and let it go at that, because it was the media they distrusted, not the President.

Not that impressions were reported as such. I would not have reported my feeling about the Nixon envy of the Russians, as based on my perception of what was in the President's mind, any more than the *Times* would have permitted it. But images and actions—all solid facts—could be collected and reported to catch the spirit of the place and convey, to some extent, what I felt deeply to be the truth. And a number of White House reporters were motivated this way.

Bias and error, of course, do creep in whenever the press

seeks to be more than a simple conveyor of information supplied by any institution. And it is made more so by the restrictions of television reporting. Newspaper reporting is much less editorial because we can make our point by laying out at length an accumulation of detail. Broadcast journalists, restricted by time and the frequent necessity to compress the most complex stories into a minute or two on the air, make the most sweeping generalizations without the corroborating facts.

For example, the broadcast reporter might say, "The mood at the White House today is one of deep gloom and pessimism" and let it go at that without stating what he based his conclusion on. But even so, the bias and error that does creep in is nowhere near as great as the great lie that would be carried abroad on many days under an uncritical relaying of the information at hand.

The White House, under any President, tends to be self-serving and often wrong. Day in and day out, it has almost every advantage to prevail over the efforts of the Washington press to ferret out the truth. The media cannot possibly find all of the wrongs and distortions and cannot sustain attack against them unless the evidence is overwhelming. A large part of the population tends to believe officials over reporters and commentators. Thus the media can exploit only the most acute of the weaknesses of anyone's White House. The remarkable thing about Nixon was that he held on as long as he did against the preponderance of damning evidence, which included the disclosures by the Senate Watergate Committee in the summer of 1973 that the Nixon White House had carried out a massive cover-up of the Watergate burglary.

Before 1973 was out, a marked change had taken place in the White House press corps since the time I had been assigned to the beat in January of that year. For years, the White House press had been accused collectively of too easily conveying the official line without the critical comment or questioning needed for accuracy and balance, for having, on occasion, too friendly and cozy relationship with White House officials, for too readily agreeing to rules established by the press office that could shape the news to the President's view, for refraining from criticism or building up an official in return for an exclusive story. Virtually all of that, however deep it may have existed among the newspaper, wire service, radio, television, and news magazine reporters, seemed to have disappeared. Some of the change undoubtedly was due to the fact that as the Watergate disclosures accumulated, suspicions and hostilities toward the press on the part of White House officials increased, and the stone wall between them and us became higher.

More than that, however, a new spirit had taken hold. Broadcast reporters in the past had not played a major role in uncovering the excesses of the White House, partly because of the regulatory power the government held over that industry. Now, with the Nixon Presidency weakened and Congress offering no obstacle, they felt free to pursue every scent of scandal and to hold officials to the harshest questioning on the air. And one by one, the large, conservative newspapers that had been avid supporters of Nixon—the *Chicago Tribune*, the *Detroit News*, the Hearst papers—defected from the Nixon cause and called for his resignation, making it easier for their reporters to do hard-nosed reporting. The new spirit stemmed, too, from the fact that most reporters felt that their right to report the news without interference had been abused over a long period of time and this was no longer to be tolerated. There was a consensus that if this spirit had existed in 1972, the American people, before they went to the polls, would have known more about what kind of people the Nixon people *were*, not just what they *did*.

8
THE SEARCH FOR A PSYCHIATRIST

"We have on good authority a report that Nixon is seeing a psychiatrist."

Those words, from an editor in New York during the Nixon stay in San Clemente in August 1973, put goose bumps on my back. The state of the President's health, physical and mental, was the unwritten story of the year. The White House line was that the President was in excellent health after a stay in Bethesda Naval Hospital for viral pneumonia in July, that, of course, he had been under a strain from the Watergate charges, but was in good spirits, determined to continue leading the country despite hordes of enemies seeking to bring him down. But the White House line was not to be trusted.

Ever since the Watergate disclosures began in the early spring, one of the daily concerns of the White House reporters had been the mood and mental health of the man under attack. Because nothing said about him by his spokesmen was to be believed, reporters felt it necessary to get a close look at him as often as possible. As a result, we would attend photo sessions or some routine ceremony in the Oval Office or the Rose Garden in search of any sign of behavior or appearance that would offer a clue to how he was holding up under the assault.

On some days he looked awful, his face appearing fatigued and heavy as he went about the routine of being President.

Occasionally, in a public speech, an expression of intense pain would sweep over his face. At other times, he appeared to be suffering from a hangover, as if light or the slightest noise hurt him. But at other times he looked surprisingly well, with a ruddy tan and lively actions. When I questioned people who had had a private audience with Nixon they usually said, "He looks great! I don't know how he does it." The search was all the more difficult because for almost every televised appearance he wore heavy makeup that camouflaged his natural complexion. Nixon was also a man physically uncoordinated, one who never seemed to be in control of his body, and he was so uncomfortable with small talk that his behavior seemed awkward. Once, when Nixon's chit-chat with a group of visiting city officials seemed to me to be totally disconnected, I had to be reminded by a long-time Nixon watcher that he was the same before Watergate.

In the late summer, however, there was a series of incidences that renewed concerns about his mental state. One such incident, involving Ron Ziegler, occurred in New Orleans, enroute to San Clemente. Nixon had spent the weekend in Key Biscayne and had stopped in New Orleans on Monday, August 20, to address the national convention of the Veterans of Foreign Wars. Before his arrival, the Secret Service had announced its agents had uncovered a "possible conspiracy" to assassinate him. Not much came of this disclosure except that the highly publicized route of the Presidential motorcade had to be changed at the last minute and the hundreds of thousands of people the Nixon advance men had expected to cheer the embattled President never saw him. For whatever reason, Nixon was in a sour mood when he arrived at the Rivergate Convention Center, even though there were friendly crowds pushing around him. As he stepped through the entrance and as Ziegler, followed by reporters and cameramen sought to follow, an expression of anger passed over Nixon's face. He grabbed Ziegler by the shoulders, spun him around and shoved him forcefully away, saying, "I don't want any press with me and you take care of it." Later, when Ziegler was asked what had gotten into the President, he said over and over, "It was nothing." But the entire ugly scene was shown repeatedly to the nation on television.

In addition to that, the President's actions were very strange as he addressed a friendly audience of war veterans and defended his order for the secret bombing of Cambodia in 1969 as necessary for saving lives and moving the war in Southeast Asia to the negotiating table. He slurred his words, he made rapid gestures, his face was flushed with excitement. The son of one of my colleagues, who was familiar with the drug scene and had watched it all on television, had a simple explanation: "He's on uppers."

The next day, Warren told reporters the President was not on medication of any kind, and his news conference of a few days later was convincing evidence that Nixon, although deeply disturbed, was very much in control of himself. His continued periods of seclusion with his family and his friend, C. G. Rebozo, however, raised suspicions all over again. There was constantly some rumor or report to run down, such as one printed by Jack Anderson that Nixon was drinking quite heavily, stout martinis made by Rebozo who would pour vermouth over ice, then pour it out and fill the glass with gin. The press office said only that the President would have a cocktail or two, in moderation.

Reporters in idle hours would sit around and imagine the worst. The worst was that the President, under unprecedented pressures and accusations, might, in a fit of irrational desperation, stage some world crisis such as a war in order to divert attention from Watergate. There was also the possibility, many of us thought at the time, that the pressures would become so unbearable that the President might attempt to end his life, even though that did not seem characteristic of Nixon. One wire service reporter had framed a bulletin in his mind for just such an occurrence. This was not just idle, morbid thinking. We had seen and covered many unanticipated disasters in recent years. It was impossible to view the Nixon Presidency without entertaining thoughts of some tragic end. Much of my own experience had been the reporting of violence, including several assassinations, urban riots, and the death and brutality associated with the civil rights movement. Furthermore, there was the fear, the wondering, of not being able to learn the truth if something should happen to the President behind the shield of security that he maintained in places such as San Clemente and Key Biscayne.

The report of Nixon seeing a psychiatrist, if true, did not mean much in itself. Perhaps it was a good sign that he was determined to sustain a semblance of mental health under pressures that not many people could withstand. If thousands of people in positions of high responsibility were under psychiatric care, and they were, there was no reason why the President of the United States, faced with the stresses of his office, should not also have such care. But the report also suggested the possibility that Nixon was more disturbed than his spokesmen indicated, and under the circumstances, it was a report we could not ignore. What I did not want to do was go to Ziegler or Warren or anyone else in the White House and ask if it were true. Such a request was sure to bring a denial, if not an angry lecture, and make it harder to confirm the report if the President indeed were under psychiatric treatment.

What was required, then, was some detective work to compile evidence that could not be repudiated by the White House. We had the name of the psychiatrist, a man prominent in medical and academic circles. The report seemed all the more promising because we were unable to find him. The *Times* distributed pictures of the doctor to their reporters so we could be on the lookout for him. We questioned guards, Secret Service agents, and others to find if a man of his description had been seen entering the White House or the Presidential compound at San Clemente. One San Clemente official said, yes, he may have seen such a person entering the compound while the President was there. When Nixon returned to Washington, I watched the President's party board the plane and searched the passenger list later, but found no such person. But this did not mean much. With its intensive security, the White House can always hide people who visit the President, and no one thought the President would have a prominent psychiatrist traveling with him so that he could be spotted by a reporter.

The search went on for weeks. It finally was abandoned after all of our leads produced nothing and the psychiatrist, who had been traveling and could not be reached any sooner, denied the report. There were other rumors about the President's health that had to be checked. One reporter in London was sent out into the English countryside to interview a noblewoman who was supposed to have some first-hand knowledge of a cabinet member's remark at a social gathering that the President was close to a breakdown. But this, too, proved to be an empty lead.

Washington, known to be a rumor factory without peer, was obsessed by talk of the President's condition—at cocktail and dinner parties, in the Capitol corridors and cloakrooms, in the departments, and in the back rooms of the White House. Small things that would not have been noticed months earlier would set off the talk—the disclosure by an unnamed Presidential aide that Nixon had been coughing blood before going into the hospital in July for viral pneumonia; a statement by the President's daughter, Julie Eisenhower, that her father had trouble getting out of bed in the mornings and sometimes would roam the White House alone and play the piano in the wee hours; the President's own statements that he would hold on to his office "as long as I am physically able."

There was ample reason for concern, both in the history of the Presidency and in the character of Richard Nixon. In the past, even before the Presidency reached its super state, medical findings and observations by Presidential physicians were overshadowed by political considerations of Presidential aides who never wanted it publicly known that the President was in a bad way. Woodrow Wilson lay near death for months while his assistants put out encouraging bulletins about the state of his health. Franklin Roosevelt was elected to a fourth term under wartime security without public awareness of the failing state of his health. If the President can do no wrong—which is standard orthodoxy among spokesmen for the modern White House —then it follows that the President cannot be subdued by the physical and mental ailments that afflict ordinary men. The physicians who attend him can be persuaded to go along through their silence or the ambiguity of their diagnoses.

Nixon, in addition to raising the unreliability of the White House press staff to an unprecedented level, was a man with a strange personal background. While almost all politicians are gregarious and like the people with whom they must constantly jostle, Nixon was a combative introvert, drawn into politics by an opportunity to run for Congress, but never showing much capacity to savor and enjoy the victories that came his way. By the time he became President, much was known about his character. He had laid much of it out in a remarkable book, *Six Crises,* written after his defeat in the 1962 California governor's race, in which he judged his life, and those of others, in the context of the ability to meet and overcome great personal challenges. By the time the Watergate scandals erupted, psychologists and psychiatrists, both amateurs and professionals, were theorizing as to how he would react to the pressures. A class in abnormal psychology at Stanford University was reported to have used the 1962 Nixon press conference, in which he said the press would no longer have Nixon to kick around, as a case study. Books purporting to analyze the Nixon mind were rolling off the presses.

Some members of Congress, which had ultimate responsibility, under the Twenty-fifth Amendment, of deciding if a President is disabled, began consulting medical authorities for their opinions of Mr. Nixon's health. The President himself deepened the mystery with statements of his spartan nature and habits and his declaration that "I am the coolest man in the room." In a rare interview, late in 1972, Nixon had said that he had such excellent health that "I never had a headache in my

life." His personal physician, Dr. Walter Tkach, said with
amazement, "I have never known a man who never had a
headache."

The last thing a reporter should try to do, I thought, was to
psychoanalyze the President, to form some conclusion about
the state of his mind and make that a theme of his reporting.
Rather, his responsibility was to watch for any signs of aberrant
behavior and report them in detail. One example of this was the
President's sixty-first birthday party, which members of his staff
arranged as a surprise in his office at San Clemente on January
9, 1973. Only a year earlier, as he entered his second term,
Nixon had confidently wielded possibly the greatest political
power held by an American President. But on this birthday,
even his supporters conceded that the most pressing question
facing him was how to survive in office. He had come to San
Clemente the day after Christmas on a commercial airliner—
an effort to avoid criticism at the height of an energy shortage
—to escape the midwinter dreariness of Washington. But since
his arrival, it had rained almost constantly, there was a minor
earthquake, the tide that washed the beaches was the highest
in three hundred years and the news was filled with reports of
mudslides and accidents.

On his birthday, the staff of twenty-five or so that accompanied him from Washington sought to cheer the boss with a
big birthday cake. Ziegler, in a misjudgment that was understandable, decided it would be good publicity to call in the
cameras and a writing pool, which I was on. While the President
was conferring with Alexander M. Haig, Jr., his chief of staff,
Mrs. Nixon and the Nixon's oldest daughter, Tricia Cox, C. G.
Rebozo, and the rest of the staff, rolled in the blue, yellow, and
white cake and struck up a squeaky "Happy Birthday." Nixon,
standing in front of his desk before a large oceanfront window,
wore a maroon jacket and gray slacks. His face seemed puffy
and weary but he smiled stiffly as the cake was placed on his
desk.

"Hey, King, want a little lick?" he called to his Irish setter,

King Timahoe, who was mingling with the crowd. After a little coaxing the dog began licking the cake with his lavish tongue, as some in the crowd laughed nervously. "He was given to me on my birthday five years ago," the President said. "He did not like cake then." In the confusion Nixon leaned against the cake and got gobs of gooey icing on his coat. "Let King lick it off," someone said. And while the President of the United States sat stiffly in his chair, the large, red dog ambled over and carried out his orders.

In the pool report, I described the scene in vivid detail. [It was the last good pool in the Nixon Presidency I was assigned to.] For my own story, I juxtaposed the birthday party with the White House ending its disclosure phase of Operation Candor —an effort to clear the President's name that had begun in November with Warren's statement that "The President is looking forward to working with Congress, the Cabinet, the American people to attack the critical issues in both foreign and domestic policy—peace in the Middle East, the energy crisis, health, housing, and manpower; he is approaching this year in a positive way"—and with the Nixons' departure for Palm Springs in a further search for the sun. While I knew this would bring charges of bias on my part, I also knew that the worst kind of distortion would be a failure to report the surrealism that was so evident in San Clemente that winter.

There seemed to be a further obligation on the part of the press to report to some degree the concern that was evident behind the scenes about the President's health. The way the news media had traditionally worked was to say nothing about the possibility of the President becoming disabled in office, while his assistants sought to keep the matter secret unless there was some legitimate development to bring it up. The subject was too delicate and the Presidency too strong an influence on the media for speculative stories on Presidential health, an example of the superficiality of White House reporting in the past. To say nothing was hardly fair to the public when much of official Washington was concerned about the subject. Rumors, even when unfounded, become legitimate news when they start to have an impact on events. I did a story for the *Times* pointing out the nature and extent of the concern and how it had become another dimension of the Watergate affair. It was written with restraint and ran inside the paper, but it served, I thought, to inform *Times* readers of a potential danger and a deeply emotional development in Washington that had gone largely unreported.

The publication of that story, on December 3, 1973, brought in another round of angry letters. From Irvington, New Jersey, a man wrote, "Your Nixon health bit was just one more assist in the national media conspiracy to overthrow the President." Again, the message was quite clear: the Presidency was not an institution to be tampered with, and what I thought was a legitimate effort to shed some light on a question of public concern was viewed by many as blasphemy.

At the same time, I felt the press has never had adequate means to properly report on Presidential health. This was pointed up to me on February 13, 1974, when Nixon, after a two-month delay for reasons that were never entirely clear, underwent his annual physical examination. Dr. Tkach, who had conducted the tests with a team of six other physicians at Bethesda Naval Medical hospital, was ecstatic about the President's excellent condition, which showed neither emotional nor physical signs of the strain he had been under for the previous months. Everything was perfect, according to Dr. Tkach. Blood pressure was 120 over 74, his pulse was 72, his weight 172, all remarkably normal for a man of 61.

The trouble was that Dr. Tkach seemed too enthusiastic, that his findings were something more than clinical. The President never overate, never overdrank, never took medication, not even tranquilizers. The only thing Tkach would recommend was for the President to get more sunshine. Because Nixon was then under criticism for making so many trips to Florida, Tkach was asked if there was medical proof that sunshine was healthy. He replied that while there was none, "It is a change in atmosphere. I think it does an individual good to know he is exposed to sunlight. He looks better when he has a suntan."

The following summer, Nixon developed phlebitis, a blood clot in the leg, a fact that he kept secret for several days until the news leaked out. Ziegler was able to keep Tkach from discussing the details with reporters for several days. Throughout this period, and later after Nixon had resigned and was hospitalized in California for several weeks, there was a question as to whether the American people were receiving correct information about his condition.

The staff of doctors who serve the President are military officers, subject to the commands of the President and other superiors. As part of the White House staff, they are subject to all of the influences and pressures that prevail in that center of high tensions, neuroses, and political motivations. Medical information, like all other emanating from the White House, should be examined with the greatest of skepticism. In reporting the President's health, however, reporters are less able to go behind the medical bulletins for the truth than in most other areas. The word of the doctors has to be taken on faith most of the time, just as reporters covering the White House under Wilson and Roosevelt accepted without any great amount of questioning what turned out to be less than adequate health information. This has given rise to various proposals, including one that Presidents be required to receive the stamp of approval from an outside panel of psychiatrists. In view of the fact that psychiatrists can disagree violently on the most basic questions and that they lack universal esteem by the public, that proposition is almost as frightening as having a disabled President at the helm. Until the Presidency drops its role as royalty and becomes simply executive government as intended by the founding fathers, perhaps the best solution is for the public to recognize that White House doctors, too, are part of the President's court and hope that somewhere in the government there will be those of sound mind to blow the whistle in the event of Presidential disability.

9
THE INSIDE VIEW

October 1973 was a remarkable month in Washington for two reasons. First, there was news a writer of fiction would never have imagined. On the tenth, Vice President Agnew resigned after pleading no contest to a charge of income tax evasion. Two days later, Nixon nominated Gerald Ford to succeed him. On the sixteenth, Melvin Laird, Nixon's domestic adviser, disclosed he had warned the President that impeachment might result if he denied the Supreme Court, which was expected to rule on lawsuits to gain possession of the White House tapes for the special prosecutor and Congress. On the nineteenth, Nixon offered his "compromise" solution—to release a summary of the tapes with Senator John C. Stennis of Mississippi verifying the accuracy of the summary. The following morning, Archibald Cox, the prosecutor, announced he would neither accept the President's proposal nor succumb to White House pressure by resigning his office, and that evening Nixon, through Ziegler, announced the firing of Cox, the abolition of his office, the resignation of Attorney General Elliott Richardson, and the firing of Richardson's deputy, William D. Ruckelshaus, for their refusals to dismiss Cox. For the remainder of the month, Washington was in an uproar.

The second remarkable thing about October was that Washington had a run of the most pleasant balmy weather it had seen in a long time, making the volcanic events at the White House seem all the more strange. Every morning, as I walked through the northwest gate and down the curved drive-way to see what new horror would unfold that day, the familiar old mansion and trees with orange leaves would be framed against the azure sky, and there was a sensuous warmth in the air that suggested a picnic of wine and cheese on the lawn, a suggestion that would have been blasphemous even in normal times. The White House has a hidden tennis court on the lawn, but a young man who had served under Lyndon Johnson told me staff members who lusted to use it never did. Presidential assistants are supposed to work long, impossible hours, even on weekends and holidays, and the amount of time spent working is a gauge of loyalty to the President and his cause, whatever that might be.

Had all of those who slaved so loyally for Richard Nixon noticed the lapse of time outside their windows? When the Watergate disclosures began to swamp the President, the first buds of spring were seen. Now the leaves were falling. The tulips in the Rose Garden had given way to a succession of summer flowers and now chrysanthemums. One of the idle occupations of White House reporters was to guess, and bet, on how long Nixon could last. There was no consensus on that. In the spring, some thought he could not last until fall, but some, who, for years, had witnessed what seemed to be the supreme authority of the President in all things, believed he would serve out his term, hobbled, but in office. I changed my mind from week to week, until the "Saturday Night Massacre," as the firing of Cox and the others came to be known.

When the news broke that evening, I was at home finishing dinner. No one had expected such a quick and drastic reaction by the President. Cox, in his press conference earlier in the day, had made such a favorable impression that it would have seemed reasonable for the President, had he valued the force of public opinion, to deal cautiously and gently with the challenge that Cox presented. By the time I reached my office, the aura of rash injustice was in the air. To my colleagues, the President's action had the flavor of a Nazi *putsch*. That was not surprising, but as I approached the White House, it became evident that this was one Nixon action that would not ever "play in Peoria," a phrase coined by John Ehrlichman to emphasize that Nixon's "middle America" had a different opinion from Eastern liberals. Angry citizens were beginning to gather on Pennsylvania Avenue in front of the White House, and members of Congress, interviewed on the radio, were reacting with disbelief.

Once inside the gate, however, I felt a remarkable change. Lights twinkled in the West Wing and in the Executive Office Building, and a full row of cars parked on Executive Avenue between the buildings indicated that it was not a normal Saturday night. But there was a hush in the warm air and I could see staff members in their offices working without any display of excitement or alarm. Most of the reporters had cleared out of the press room. From the *Times'* cubbyhole I got Ziegler on the telephone without having to wait. He talked in a routine manner, describing the action as a logical sequence of events in which the President had acted in a most reasonable way. On the outside, people were wondering if the President had lost his mind; on the inside, the question was: What is all the fuss about? And this seemed to be a genuine feeling, not pretense.

The next day, Sunday, October 21, the feeling was the same, but I knew the White House people were anxious to have their version of the events known when Alexander M. Haig, Jr., agreed to see me that very day. Haig, who had taken Haldeman's place as chief of staff, was not like the rest of the Nixon people. He was a career army officer who had served, in the first Nixon term, on the national security staff for Kissinger. His three stars were all earned in the White House, but early in 1973 he was happy to go back to the Pentagon as deputy army chief of staff, and he aspired to be the chief. Yet when Nixon called him back, in early May, to replace Haldeman, he had no choice but to serve the man who had so rapidly elevated him in rank.

A good case could have been made that General Haig, before his retirement from active duty on August 1, served illegally as Nixon's chief of staff. A section of the United States Code forbids a military officer from holding a "civil office." Senator Stuart Symington, the Missouri Democrat who had served as Air Force secretary, said he doubted the President had the right to turn the office of the President into "a military command without Congressional authority." Representative John E. Moss, Democrat of California, sought to make a capital case of the appointment, arguing, even after General Haig's retirement, that both the law and the tradition of civilian control over the military had been violated. Yet not much attention was paid to all of this. The country had become accustomed to the President, whoever he was, doing pretty much what he wanted despite tradition and legal technicalities; writing the law as he went along on such matters as executive privilege and impoundment of funds. Nixon's spokesmen shrugged off the objections as petty interference.

Haig, I thought, was a man of some conscience and a sense of the public interest. He suited Nixon because he had a military mind, could execute orders, keep the staff in line, and serve as the one-man conduit Nixon wanted to communicate with the rest of the world. Haig was frightening to some because he was a general serving as assistant President in the seat of power reserved for civilian control. Those who knew him would have trusted him with the bomb over some of the civilians Nixon had in high authority. I did not think Haig had a grasp of politics, but then Nixon was considered the ultimate political expert on all matters, and we had had enough of political wizards.

In any event, Haig was not paranoid about the press the way most of the Nixon people were. He saw reporters regularly. He tried to make the White House more open, and I was always under the impression that if Haig had had his way, Ziegler would not have been press secretary. Haig, however, probably because of his military background, was extraordinarily cautious, and what he said in the few private interviews I had with him rarely made news. He was valuable for insights and impressions, which, as I have said before, served the reporter during this period better than words or disclosures.

Most of the White House offices had emptied by Sunday afternoon. To get to Haig I had to stop by the Executive Office Building and the office of Ken W. Clawson, the communications director who was working with Haig in an effort to improve the President's public relations, and pick up an escort for entry into the West Wing. When I finally arrived, after having to go through checkpoints, down long halls, and up an elevator, I felt as if I was in the inner sanctum. The chief of staff's office, down the hall from the President's Oval Office, is on the southwest corner and looks out on the ellipse and the Executive Office Building.

As I noted earlier, it is tradition for a Presidential assistant, when he occupies an office, to have it made over with furnishings and colors to suit his own taste, frequently in a matter of hours, and without regard to cost. Haig, however, did not do this. The office was as Haldeman left it. The dominating feature was a somber gray woodwork that made the room seem quite heavy. Haig was cordial, although his eyes were red and weary. His explanation, which went a few steps beyond Ziegler's, was that the President had made an offer that was most generous. Every effort had been made to accommodate Cox, but he had persistently resisted all White House efforts for a settlement and "no President could have accepted that kind of defiance."

The point that Haig stressed over and over was that the President had decided to give in because he saw the continuance of the tapes dispute as damaging to the country. Some foreign nations were beginning to see a weakened United States. The President was unwilling to stand for this, so he was willing to compromise much further than any of his aides had ever expected. If Cox did not like it, he could have resigned. The resignation of Richardson was a loss to the administration, but it was one that could be overcome. Mr. Cox's argument that he could not accept the compromise because it contained the means of blocking him from the evidence he needed, was discounted as irrelevant.

The interview was interrupted several times by Nixon summoning Haig to his office. Haig would spring to his feet, stand ramrod straight, button his jacket, and march off at a fast clip. He would be gone for what seemed a long time. While he was away, I tried to understand what he had said, while I looked out the stately windows and examined the banks of telephone buttons that kept Alexander Haig in touch with the world. After a time, I began to see things in his perspective. Here was the center of power of probably the most powerful nation of the world. From these offices the President could and did command his armies, his navies, his big bombers, his two and a half million civil servants. He could and did reshape the Supreme Court and appointed judges across the land. He could and did structure, according to his own philosophy, the regulatory agencies that had once been an arm of Congress. He could and did hold Congress under his control. Around the world—and it was this that seemed to improve the Nixon aides the most—the President was on the verge of bringing about an order of peace, they sincerely thought, while at home, mischievious men were nipping at his heels.

The crowds out on Pennsylvania Avenue seemed a long way off, even though in the White House you could hear the horns of automobiles responding to the signs in the crowd that read: "Honk for Impeachment." It was nothing; people were always demonstrating for something on Pennsylvania Avenue. There had been half a million people demonstrating against the war early in the Nixon reign and a moat of busses kept them back. The voices of protest from Congress seemed thin. They were, as Melvin Laird had said on "Meet the Press" that day, mostly "the same ones who opposed us on Vietnam." The President could ride it out. It would be over in a few days. An American President could be sure of his term. He was not like those European parlimentary leaders who could be tossed out by ripples of public opinion.

Responsibility seemed to weigh heavily on Alexander Haig that day. He would say later that the Cox firing set off a "fire storm" that was not easily endured. He cautioned me as I left, that the newspapers, which had been stirring things up for months, had a responsibility, too, to remain cool.

It was not until I walked out the northeast gate and became part of the outside world again that I realized how wide was the gap between the inside view and the outside view. Setting aside rationalizations and self-serving attitudes, which were legion, it seemed that the Nixon people day after day underestimated the seriousness of the opposition.

It was not merely the paranoid attitudes of Richard Nixon and some of his associates. The modern White House changes its people in basic ways. There they are the vortex of a super Presidency that has been at work most of this century. They come to think of the White House as the center of the universe. Congress becomes a center of buffoons, who neither toil hard enough nor stand up to political pressures. The media is recklessly irresponsible. The courts can go off on wild and irresponsible tangents. But the Presidency is there to restore wisdom, stability, and balance. The White House people, then, are caught up in history. They must capture the moment, working during every waking moment to make the most of it. Life that goes on outside is mundane.

These feelings were so intense by those close to President Nixon, that the most mature and level-headed were rarely listened to because they were thought to be much too influenced by outside forces. Foxy old Melvin Laird, whose years in Congress and brushes with all kinds of people gave him some immunity to White House influences, had his recommendations turned down so often that he ultimately committed a heresy: he went public in the sense that he would leak his frustrations to columnists he had known over the years.

Yet the overseriousness with which the Nixon people took themselves seemed to spread to everyone involved. George Shultz, who was Nixon's economic czar for much of his term, was quoted by William Safire in his book, *Before the Fall,* as follows: "What a waste. In the first term we discovered where the levers were, how to actually change the direction of power away from Washington. And then we had to go through the price control business and that was out of our system. Here was a new term, a real mandate, a chance to put some good ideas into action. Now it's all gone up in smoke [because of Watergate]. We had it in our hands to do such great, sound things, in the way that was right for the country. We had it right in our hands. . . ." Only the Nixon people could be Messianic about leading the country away from Messianic influences.

Outside the White House, the view of the "Saturday Night Massacre" turned out to be the correct one. Nixon did "tough it out" and show some signs of rallying thereafter. But it made the previously unthinkable idea of impeachment thinkable and respectable. It caused Nixon to lose some of his bedrock support as conservative newspapers, journalists, and political leaders defected over the next few days. Cox was succeeded by Leon Jaworski, a tough and pragmatic Texas lawyer who turned out to be a tougher prosecutor than Cox. Jaworski's appointment had the approval of the White House. The Nixon people, who never understood southerners, thought he would be less aggressive than Cox because he was part of the Texas Democratic conservative establishment. What they overlooked was the fact that Jaworski had once been a controversial figure in his own state—an advocate of unpopular causes—and was now accepting a place in history.

One day in early November, after the balm of October had passed and as a cold rain pattered on the pavement outside the White House press room, I asked Helen Thomas of UPI, whose judgment about Nixon I most respected, what she thought. "It's all over," she said, her dark eyes more serious than usual. "This is a death watch." Betting on the question of how long could he last was no longer fun. The contest now for White House reporters was to try to find ways to measure the pulse of a dying Presidency.

10
CAN A PRESS SECRETARY SUCCEED?

After the "Saturday Night Massacre" there was a marked increase in weird and mysterious White House developments, which further indicated a terminal malady. There was the disclosure of the eighteen-minute gap in a crucial tape recorded conversation between Nixon and Haldeman on June 20, 1972, three days after the Watergate break-in, with Rose Mary Woods' tortured efforts in federal court to explain it away and Haig's assessment that "some sinister force" was at work; there was "Operation Candor" in which Nixon sought to open himself up on Watergate before members of Congress and the public to clear his name but only mired deeper in the contradictions; there was the unprecedented disclosure of Nixon's income tax returns for his first four years in office which raised more charges about his personal finances; there was his remarkable disclaimer of November 17 before a news conference at Disney World, Florida, that "I'm not a crook;" there was his sudden abandonment of "the imperial Presidency" at Christmas time when, as earlier related, he took a commercial plane to San Clemente to save energy, only to resume his lavish mode of travel a few weeks later after some friends in Congress were reported to have told him he should act like a President. And on it went.

Between the waves of seemingly aberrant behavior, Nixon would show signs of renewal and vigor. James D. St. Clair, a respected Boston barrister and Nixon's new attorney on Watergate matters, gave the President a boost in the courts and in Congress with defensive legal tactics that seemed, for a time, very promising. Nixon could still draw the crowds and partisan support, if he picked his places for public appearances carefully, as he did. In Huntsville, Alabama, on February 18, Nixon was greeted by George C. Wallace, in a wheel chair, and a friendly crowd of 20,000 at an "Honor America Day" rally. After five days in Florida he was looking healthy and confident. The old, combative Nixon once again slashed away at his opponents, at least catching the imagination of those faithful legions in Huntsville, a space center made up mostly of federal employees. In a "what's right with America" speech, Nixon said, "In the nation's capital there is a tendency for partisanship to take over from statesmanship. In the nation's capital there is a tendency in the reporting of news—I do not say this critically, it's simply a fact of life—that bad news is news and good news is not news. And as a result, those of us who work there and try to develop the policies of the nation may get a distorted view of what is America and what it is really like."

On March 16, Nixon flew to Nashville, Tennessee, to help dedicate the new home of the Grand Ole Opry and to cement his support by a segment of "middle America" that somehow found Richard Nixon appealing. Nixon is most remembered in that appearance by his futile effort to master the yo-yo Roy Acuff had handed him on stage. Nixon's return to the political campaign—a campaign to hold on to his public support—was better demonstrated in his appearance at the Tennessee Air National Guard Hangar which had all the trappings of a rally shortly before an election: crowds, banners, bands, advance men, oratory, and patriotism. To add to the drama, Air Force One, in all its gleaming splendor, pulled right up to the hangar where Tennessee Republicans and White House technicians had been at work for days to stage the event for its maximum effectiveness. When he arrived, the crowd sang from mimeographed sheets:

STAND UP AND CHEER FOR RICHARD NIXON

(Tune—"Okie from Muscogee")

Now I'm not from Muscogee, Oklahoma,
But I believe in right and being free.
I'm sick of what I'm reading in the papers,
I'm tired of all that trash that's on TV.

(Chorus)
Stand up and cheer for Richard Nixon,
For he's the President of our great land.
We said we wanted peace and we got it,
He brought our soldiers home from Vietnam.

I've been hearing talk about impeaching,
The man we chose to lead us through these times.
But talk like this could weaken and defeat us,
Let's show the world we're not the quitting kind.

All of this could be very confusing, with Nixon one day down and out and the next seemingly in charge of the situation. It became more important than before to report what the President and his assistants *were* as well as what they *did*. This could be done, for my purposes, only with a rendition of the evidence from which the reader could draw his own conclusions. I thought I detected beneath all the veneer of self-confidence and assertiveness of the President, Haig, Ziegler, and others, signs that most of the time they really did not know what to do. Robert B. Semple, Jr., who preceded me as a *Times* White House reporter, had told me, when I first took the assignment, not to look too much for substance and design, that frequently, when he would try to find and define some grand strategy, the trail led nowhere. As Gertrude Stein was reported to have said on seeing Oakland, California, "There's not much *there* there." The Great Oz would turn out to be only a bumbler. This was not true of Nixon himself. He was an intelligent and complex man capable of conceptual thinking, and his innovations in foreign policy were in some respects quite remarkable and well thought out. But on domestic policies and other areas, that which was seen on the surface was all there was. The White House tapes were later to confirm the uncertainty and desperation on Watergate matters.

In the winter and spring before release of the tapes, it seemed important to document the bankruptcy of the Nixon efforts to hold on to office. In his own writings, Nixon had described the importance he placed on the counterattack. With a little research, I found that by the end of 1974 Nixon had carried out eight phases of counterattack: (1) he was the detective who promised to find the truth and see that justice is done; (2) he accepted responsibility and shook up his government; (3) he sought to protect himself with the national security issue; (4) he moved to show he had opened his administration to Congress and the public; (5) he tried to show he was preoccupied with the government's business while others "wallow in Watergate"; (6) he showed himself to the American people as harrassed and abused by the media; (7) doubling back to (5), he tried to show the President "doing something" in the way of government business to prove his indispensibility; (8) he opened himself up to the courts and Congress—partially, it turned out—in what the media tagged, without objections from the White House, "Operation Candor." A simple rendering of each phase in a 1,000-word story showed, I thought, the Great Oz fumbling quite desperately for any lever that might work.

As the end neared, and after one strategy after the other failed, the Nixon people put more and more stress on showing that the government was working quite well and quite normally despite the Watergate charges and the impeachment proceedings underway on Capitol Hill. This was where Ken W. Clawson came in. Clawson was a former *Washington Post* reporter who had joined the administration in the first term when Charles W. Colson was running the Office of Communications. Nixon had established the office early in his administration, under Herbert G. Klein, his long-time press aide, in order to by-pass the regular Washington press and make direct contact with publishers and broadcasters across the nation. Some of the harsher Nixon critics said at the time they knew of no non-totalitarian nation with a function called the Office of Communications. It turned out to be very effective, especially in the reelection campaign when Colson took charge and made it part of his hard sales pitch for Nixon.

Clawson was there as acting director—Klein turned out to be too much of a gentlemen to cut it in the Nixon White House —when Haig came in. In the winter and into the spring of 1974, the press briefings with Warren, and occasionally with Ziegler, had deteriorated into nasty snarls in which not much was communicated. To show what I mean, the following exchange is from a Ziegler briefing of May 6, after the White House transcripts made disclosures that seemed to conflict with Ziegler statements of the past:

Q: Did you have any problem coming out and telling us things that really weren't true?

A: I said from this podium what I felt to be the developments as they did occur, and I would call your attention to the fact that the transcripts do show Mr. Dean was sent to Camp David to prepare a report.

Q: So you would argue, then, with the assertion that you were telling us stuff that wasn't true?

A: I would state to you that we did not come out here with the overt attempt to state things that I felt were not as they were.

Q: You don't feel compromised personally by the release of these transcripts? [the transcripts showed White House officials carrying out a cover-up of Watergate at the time Ziegler was publicly denying any existence of a cover-up.]

A: No, I don't.

In view of that state of affairs in Ziegler's office, Haig gave Clawson authority to carry out a separate public relations drive, not only with the media outside Washington, but with the Washington press as well. Except for his loyalty to Nixon, Clawson was nothing like Ziegler. A chubby man with owlish eyes and a raspy voice, he was an Appalachian mountaineer who had come up from poverty. He was a hard-nosed reporter who became a bare-knuckles fighter within the administration. Some reporters scorned him as a street fighter who would go for the groin. But when it came to choosing between Clawson and Ziegler, I much preferred Clawson. Whatever his service for Richard Nixon, he thought for himself and he was not plastic like Ziegler. He had experienced hard knocks in life, perhaps too many, and there was no pretense about him. One day he wandered through the press room shouting, "Does anyone want a piece of Chuck Connors?" That was his way of asking if anyone wanted to interview the cowboy actor who was in the White House to see the President. Clawson knew what reporters needed and wanted. He expected to be punched and he liked to punch back.

Clawson and his staff of ten occupied a corner suite of offices in the old Executive Office Building, looking out on Executive and Pennsylvania Avenues. In the effort to show that the government was functioning normally, Clawson set up interviews with various White House officials and cabinet members in one of his offices and invited various reporters and columnists to attend. At first, these were held at 5 P.M., and Clawson served cocktails in an effort to avoid some of the poison that flowed in the White House press room where Ziegler was in charge. These sessions got to be known as "Cocktails with Clawson" and drew considerable criticism, as almost everything in the executive government did in those days. The sessions were dismissed by some as simply another way to finagle the public through reporters who were being taken in by the Clawson operation.

To me, however, most of the sessions in the stuffy, baby-blue carpeted room were another window into the dying Presidency. There was rarely a spot news story in them on a positive aspect of government. Rather than displaying the administration as being viable and active, they more often documented the bankruptcy. Casper W. Weinberger, secretary of Health,

Education and Welfare, would disclose, under intensive questioning, that initiatives in welfare reform and national health insurance were no longer underway. Nothing was happening. Secretary of Agriculture Earl T. Butz indirectly confirmed the administration was engaged in "impeachment politics" in the sense that he and other officials were shaping policies and aid for Nixon supporters in Congress. "I make assessments myself as to who our friends are on the Hill," Butz said. "I do not go out of the way to favor those who are against us."

It would have been difficult to find one story that would have told more about the character of the Nixon administration than the May 9 interview in Clawson's office with Dr. John McLaughlin, the Jesuit priest who was a special assistant to Nixon. While some administration officials were admitting privately that the White House tapes, which had been released a few days earlier, were very damaging to the President, McLaughlin, in an exercise in convoluted logic, insisted that "the President acquitted himself throughout these discussions with honor."

While Mr. Clawson's purpose was to conduct what he called "some P.R." for the defense of Nixon, in my view, he succeeded instead in exposing some monumental defects in the Nixon regime. But his purposes did not matter so much. Through background and training, Clawson believed in granting access to reporters and this is what a press secretary's role is all about.

One of the questions I am most frequently asked by students and others who show an interest in the White House, is what should the White House press secretary be; how should he operate? The fact that there have been so few successful press secretaries in recent years is testimony to the difficult role that it is. It is difficult because under the vaunted Presidency, the demands on him are never-ending and frequently conflicting. There is no way to please everyone involved. To function at all he must first please the President, because without his own access to and trust by the President he cannot convey the information that the media expects from him. He has several constituencies in the media. The photographers want access for the picture story. The radio broadcasters want a new development for the next news on the hour. The newspapers, television, and wire service reporters want various kinds of access and information. He must deal not only with the White House press but with, in time, almost every bureau chief and reporter in town. The President wants his side of the story, his slant on the development to predominate in the media, and there are many things he does not want known at all. Yet the press secretary must also deal with the President's staff, and they can be as demanding, as devious, and as difficult as the President. Under the modern concept of the super Presidency, there is no way a press secretary can make everyone happy.

What he must do, beyond having an efficient organization and being a person with depth of character, intelligence, and experience, is to have two strong loyalties: one to the President and one to the public; because these frequently are in conflict, he must expect to live much of his life as a schizophrenic. While I have never been in government service and cannot speak for the other side, I have seen, though not often, that rare person who, in offices below the Presidency, managed to serve both the public, by providing access and disclosures, and the basic interest of his boss at the same time. One of these extraordinary people is Joseph Laitin, who for many years was press officer for the Office of Management and Budget before becoming assistant secretary of Defense for public affairs. I think the reasons he succeeded were because he was able to convince a succession of bosses that their interest and the public interest was usually the same and he made publicity-shy budget officials available to reporters. At the same time, he found ways to put his boss in the best possible light.

To be sure, the White House press secretary faces larger hurdles in functioning this way. He must find ways to reveal information that some or many on the inside do not want revealed for frivolous or self-protective reasons, and he must be willing to quit if he sees the corruption of the institution grow-ing out of control. On the other hand, if this very unusual person is going to succeed, reporters must realize, which they seldom do, that their interests are never going to be fully served by one whose loyalties have to be divided. Because the Presidency has been so overly exalted in recent years, there is a tendency to forget that the White House Press secretary is first of all a flack, which is journalistic jargon for a press agent.

In covering most agencies or institutions, reporters fre-quently find it advantageous to by-pass the press officer and go directly to the people who are making policy or administering programs. The trouble with the White House is that every re-porter, whether he wants to be or not, is dependent on the press secretary and his staff for many things. He can develop his own sources and talk to White House officials without going through the press office, but during a crisis or when the President is traveling, the officials involved, for various reasons, cannot be reached, and the one source of information may well be the press secretary. He is like the neck of the hourglass: if the sand spilling through him is not sufficient, as it frequently is not, the reporters at the bottom rant and rave. It should not be this way, but it is, another aspect of the corporate Presidency that has developed in recent years.

When reporters were raging at Ziegler, I used to hear from the old-timers that there had not been a good press secretary since James C. Hagerty, who served Eisenhower. Hagerty was good, I was told, because he held the confidence of the Presi-dent and his staff to such a great extent that he frequently made policy, on the spot, which the President subsequently endorsed. I doubt that Hagerty would be quite as successful today, be-cause of the enormous distrust that reporters have of the official line emanating from almost any office in Washington. Perhaps there is too much cynicism, but in recent years there has been such a tendency—indeed, a habit—on the part of officials throughout the government to obfuscate, if not to lie, that any-thing less than deep skepticism on the part of reporters would be dereliction of duty.

Early in 1974, I wrote an article for the *Times'* magazine which said rather clearly that because the Nixon White House had been so weakened by Watergate, the Office of Management and Budget (OMB) had moved in and was holding the government together. The interesting thing was that none of the many officials I interviewed for the article ever made that admission. On the contrary, what the officials said, in order not to appear disloyal to the President, was to stress normalcy. My conclusion came from listening between the lines and from my own observations. If I had not known the ways of official Washington and followed what the officials said, I would have been completely wrong. As it was, the article was so right that OMB had it duplicated for distribution to students and others who were interested in the role of the agency.

Since Hagerty's day, too, the White House staff has become larger and more bureaucratic, even though it was Eisenhower who took the small informal staff that Truman and previous Presidents maintained and made it larger and more like the army staff system that Eisenhower had known in the military. Subsequent Presidents, particularly Johnson and Nixon, added to it, until the President now operates with a personal staff of more than five hundred, and this does not include Presidential agencies such as the OMB, the National Security Council, and others. Furthermore, Kennedy's tendency to make the Presidency into Camelot added to the mystique of royalty that Americans seem too anxious to accept, and Johnson's deviousness and Vietnam policies and Nixon's Watergate brought a neurosis to the place that is not easily eliminated.

There was no way a press secretary could succeed under Nixon, and perhaps that was why Ziegler had the job and kept it until the end, even though some on the White House staff wanted him replaced and some of his functions were parceled off to Warren and Clawson. Yet I never was angry for long at Ziegler or blamed him for his failures; rather, I blamed the President and Haldeman for putting him in that position before he was thirty. George Reedy, who served for a time as press secretary for Lyndon Johnson, recorded his insights about the institution in *Twilight of the Presidency* and other writings. Reedy believes that no one under forty, who has not had the hard knocks of life, ought to be allowed to work in any position of importance in the White House. It is too heady an experience and it is nothing like the life he will live for the remainder of his years on the outside.

Joe Laitin, who worked in and around the White House for many years, told me once that he discouraged the very young from being there. He did not think the young should be exposed to the infighting and the power plays that are employed every day to accomplish some purpose but which, if recorded, would seem obscene. Put another way, there is a bureaucrat in Washington who is said to stand at his desk in some distant agency and click his heels whenever his secretary tells him, "The White House is calling." No matter that the caller might be a junior assistant without authority. He might be calling for the President, and the junior assistant, whether he is or not, will soon take on lordly ways.

Ziegler was a product of Southern California, which more than any other area of the United States, seems to turn out people without strong moorings or identity. He was a junior account executive for an advertising firm before he became part of the Nixon entourage. He had some strong points: a quick mind and friendly instincts, but he was given too difficult a job in the White House at too early an age and was quickly absorbed by the Nixon–Haldeman mentality. Clawson, although not much older than Ziegler, was a person of wide experience who matured before he arrived at the White House. He was more like Pat Buchanan, the pugnacious right-wing speech writer who wanted the press to be nothing more than a mindless conveyor of the President's words and actions. Both had gotten ahead under Nixon in part by attacking the media, but a reporter could at least communicate with them.

Gerald Warren, as the daily press briefer during the period of bizarre White House behavior, was a punching bag, constantly absorbing blows from the press on one side, and from

White House people who did not take him into their confidence on some crucial matters, on the other. Warren had been city editor of the *San Diego Union,* and a good one I was told by reporters who worked under him. On a very conservative, cautious paper, they said, he quietly found a way to present news of the public interest that might be blocked by the management. He did not get aroused by the pressures and was at all times patient with very nasty questions. But he was not of much help in arriving at the truth. I could not read him as I could Ziegler to see the trend of Nixon's thinking, because he was not that much in Nixon's confidence and to his own credit, he was not an extension of Nixon, as Ziegler was.

Everyone has strengths and weaknesses. The mark of a good leader is the ability to bring out the strengths and minimize the weaknesses of his subordinates. The people the press dealt with daily in the White House during the Watergate period were essentially of sound character. They certainly were not evil. Some were highly motivated. But each, I thought, displayed his worst characteristics, and part of this, I am sure, was due to a very difficult and contentious press. But the display of weaknesses over strengths was evident throughout the Nixon White House, with the exception of a few rare individuals. As the Nixon excesses became more evident, I kept waiting for someone to resign with a strong public statement of indignation. But that never happened. A few people left quietly out of disgust, preferring not to seem disloyal. To the end, Nixon had a strange hold on people who had cast their lot with him and he left in his wake, I thought, a mass of human misery and failure.

11
CONTROLLING
THE PRESS

In the spring of 1974, Nixon had one ace left, or so it seemed. That was his mastery of foreign affairs, his ability to lead the world into a new era of order and peace. To play his hand effectively, it was important to show that Nixon himself was an indispensible instrument in continuing the foreign policy initiatives of the first term—détente with Russia and China, establishment of a permanent peace in the Middle East, the re-establishment of friendly relations with old allies in Europe and Eastern Asia. Thus, 1974 would be a year of world travels for the President, to Europe, the Middle East, Russia, and Japan. Only the trip to Japan, planned for late in the year, was not carried out before Nixon's hole card paled beside the royal flush held by Congress and the courts. In the process, however, Nixon showed what an enormous control even a dying Presidency has over the media.

The death of French President Georges Pompidou in April gave Nixon an unexpected opportunity to confer with other world leaders who, like Nixon, went to Paris to pay their respects and attend a memorial service in Notre Dame Cathedral on April 6. It appeared in Washington, before his departure, that the trip would be routine in view of the fact that protocol would not permit any heavy bargaining in Paris during a period of national grieving. Because of this and the fact that the trip came on the weekend when the Gridiron Club was holding its annual banquet—an archaic social function in which journalists roast public figures in an evening of camaraderie—only a few journalists signed up to go. Because the *Times* always covers the President on any trip out of the Washington area, and it seemed like an opportunity for a pleasant weekend in Paris, where I had never been, I had no hesitancy in putting my name on the list. As it turned out, Nixon dominated the news that weekend, a development that seemed totally calculated.

When Nixon departed from Andrews Air Force Base for Paris, Watergate and related matters had dominated the news for a year. The House Judiciary Committee was well into its impeachment inquiry and was in a dispute with the White House on its efforts to obtain tape recordings and documents. On the day of his departure, April 5, Dwight L. Chapin, who had been Nixon's appointments secretary, was convicted in United States District Court of lying to a grand jury about his knowledge of campaign sabotage.

Paris was an instant relief from all of this. The Watergate charges had never been much understood outside the United States, and in France only the more politically sophisticated were beginning to understand the severity of the corruption involved and the extent of the trouble facing the President. Nixon was known around the world for his foreign policy initiatives, not as the conniving politician many at home saw him to be. Even the reporters found the change refreshing. A siege of cold rain had given way to misty sunshine and the people of Paris were out in great numbers on Saturday, strolling under newly leafed trees and pear blossoms. Great crowds milled about the cathedral, and it appeared for a time that the bus carrying the American reporters would not be able to penetrate close enough to get us to the ceremony.

At home, Secret Service agents are accustomed to ordering people around at will on behalf of the President, so much so that the agency was involved in lawsuits filed by citizens who felt their civil liberties had been violated by crowd-control tactics which, under the Haldeman rule during the first term, had become somewhat excessive. But the French police were not impressed either by the Secret Service or the credentials of the White House press. It was refreshing to watch. I was in no rush to get to the cathedral because I knew that Nan Robertson of the *Times'* Paris bureau, one of the best color writers anywhere, was there to write the ceremony. After shuttling from one corner to another, we disembarked and, through a circuitous route, finally arrived at a side entrance. Like so many hunchbacks with our baggage of recording devices, flight bags, and typewriters, we scrambled up dusty circular stone steps to the high balconies just in time for the arrival of the dignitaries and some of the most beautiful choral music I had ever heard. Nixon, in a dark gray morning coat, and seated on the front row amid other world leaders, seemed a distant, unimportant figure in the ancient and moving ceremony.

Having paid his respects, the President of the United States ordinarily would have retired and, at the most, held quiet conferences with some of the other leaders on this day of mourning. Instead, Ziegler announced Nixon would stay over an extra day, until Sunday, for high-level talks on various aspects of foreign policy. At the residence of the American Embassy, an elegant mansion built in 1842 on the Rue de Faubourg Saint Honoré, with considerable fanfare, Nixon received the leaders one by one—Prime Minister Wilson of Britain, Chancellor Willy Brandt of West Germany, President Nikolai V. Podgorny of the Soviet Union, Premier Kakuei Tanaka of Japan, and others. General Haig, when asked if Nixon had found his relations with these leaders weakened by Watergate, said, on the contrary, the prospects of Nixon's impeachment "is something that is very difficult for them to conceive of. If there was any consistent theme coming out of this visit, it is that American leadership, vitality, relevance, and participation in world affairs are vital, and a viable Presidency is a cornerstone of world security."

Between sessions, Nixon would go out on the streets and greet the friendly crowds of Parisians. A young Frenchman, who wore an American flag on his lapel, just as Nixon almost always did, approached the visiting celebrity and said, "God bless you, Mr. President." Nixon replied, "Well, God bless you." At one point Nixon, never good at small talk, asked a line of policemen holding back the crowds, "Do you like your job?" As he was leaving, shortly before noon on Sunday, there was this exchange with a crowd outside the American Embassy, from the official transcript:

THE PRESIDENT: *Au revoir.* I will come again.

A very warm good-by and a beautiful day, but we had a very good visit with our friends from France. Of course, we couldn't go into many matters because of the occasion, but also, it was an opportunity to see many other people from around the world. But we always like to come to Paris.

I look forward to coming back some day, when I have many hours, as a tourist, to try the restaurants again.

Forty years ago, I majored in French, had four years of French. After four years, I could speak it, I could write it. I read all of the classics. And today, I just understand a little.

QUESTION: When do you come back to France, Mr. President?

THE PRESIDENT: Any time I have a good excuse. I love it. Good-by. *Merci.*

On the plane back to Washington, General Haig, summarizing the trip, said, "It was very evident that European leaders and world leaders with whom the President met continue to look to the United States and President Nixon as an essential factor in the realization of the continuing efforts to develop a structure for stable international environment." Yet he did not point to any agreement reached or any specific subject on which progress was made. It was clear to the reporters that the President had been campaigning in the streets of Paris as he had been in the Grand Ole Opry a few weeks earlier. In Paris, there were not even the "impeach Nixon" signs seen everywhere he went in the United States to mar the positive effect on American television screens. Perhaps he would have done this had it not been for the Watergate charges, but I do not think so. After he left, there was bitter criticism among the French about him taking to the streets and holding policy talks on a day of national mourning.

In any event, the media in the United States played the story seriously, as substantive foreign policy talks. In my own stories, I put in as much material as I could pointing up the campaign aspects. But the thrust of the coverage everywhere, as far as I could determine, was of Nixon as world leader being cheered by foreign citizens and talking policy with other world leaders. For two days, the White House was able to focus attention away from Watergate. Returning to the United States and the daily barrage of accusations must have been a bitter experience for the President. He went immediately to Camp David for a rest.

The trip to the Middle East provided a better and longer respite from the troubles of Watergate for Nixon and his staff. In releasing the Watergate tapes, which turned out to be far from the complete story of Watergate, as he said, Nixon had made another gross misjudgment about the sensibilities of the American people. It was true that he acknowledged the documents would be embarrassing to him and that he expected a wave of criticism. But there was no indication that anyone in the White House had anticipated another fire storm like that set off by the "Saturday Night Massacre." But the reaction was almost as strong. Nixon one more time had hoped to cut his losses and put the Watergate charges behind him. There were demands from Congress and from special prosecutor Leon Jaworski for even more tapes and documents. Nixon got his back up and once again invoked executive privilege. Demands for impeachment by this time not only were respectable, they were steamrolling. On June 10, Nixon left all this behind and took off for the Middle East, landing first in Salzburg enroute and declaring that he was on what "we hope will be another journey for peace," a term he had used for his missions to China and the Soviet Union in 1972.

On what was scheduled to be a day of rest before flying to Cairo, Kissinger upset the President's plan to turn attention away from Watergate. In an extraordinary news conference at which he appeared choked with hurt and anger, Kissinger threatened to resign unless he was cleared of accusations that he participated in "illegal or shady activity" in the government's wiretapping of individuals. He also upset the plans of reporters to relax in preparation of what was to be an arduous trip. Once in Cairo, however, except for Kissinger's pouting and Nixon giving him the cold shoulder in public meetings, the explosion at Salzburg was forgotten as the American Presidency took charge as only it can.

Whatever gloom must have encompassed Richard Nixon's mind in the subsequent lonely days of forced retirement in San Clemente, the reception he received in Egypt must have remained in his memory as one of the most warming experiences of his long career. President Anwar el-Sadat, anxious to improve relations with the United States after years of uneasy dependence on the Soviet Union, turned out his people, not by the hundreds of thousands but by the millions. Transported to the parade routes by trucks and every other mode of transportation available to them, the volatile and outgoing Egyptians, thought it great fun to cheer the American President. They hung from the trees, balconies, rooftops, crowded the streets with banners, red flowers, and branches shouting, "Nick-SON! Nick-SON!" The reaction was the same through the streets of Cairo and Alexandria, and in the towns and on the lush farms in the Nile Delta, where the two presidents traveled by limousine and by train in a two-day spectacular that probably could not have been duplicated in scope and enthusiasm anywhere else.

From then on, until Nixon's return to the United States on June 19, it was like the old days. Ziegler, who had been helpless over the past year to get any sustained favorable publicity for his boss, was jubilant. If Watergate was little understood in Paris, it was not understood at all in the Arab countries, and in Israel, the dependency of that country on the United States had been so prolonged and the gratitude toward Nixon so great for his support in the past that the leaders seemed anxious to put aside any mention of the President's troubles. The power of the American Presidency, even a dying one, was on display everywhere. There were the blue and silver Presidential jets and three big cargo planes that carried five limousines for the Presidential party. Fleets of helicopters were provided from American aircraft carriers in the Mediterranean. Scores of advance men and Secret Service agents worked the cities days in advance. In what appeared to be a casual gesture of friendship, Nixon made Sadat a gift of a fifteen-million-dollar jet.

Any initiative that was underway through normal diplomatic channels was saved for the trip to make it appear a result of the President's visit, as in Damascus, where it was announced that diplomatic relations with Syria, broken since 1967, were restored. The trip as a demonstration of what Kissinger and presumably Nixon were trying to do—bring the Arab countries, as well as Israel, into the American orbit so that the United States could control peace and make its influence better felt in the region—was both fascinating and worthy of major news coverage. Yet the trip, with all of its fanfare, obscured much of the substance of what was going on, the role Nixon was able to play in his weakened condition, and to what extent whatever progress being made was dependent on Kissinger.

The White House reporters, captives of the colorful caravan, certainly could not tell. They were consumed by the ceaseless ceremony, by the long days and nights aboard buses and planes, by parades, state dinners, and airport ceremonies.

There was the constant concern with communications needed to get the endless story back to the United States. In the press room at the Kendera Palace Hotel, in Jidda, Saudi Arabia, there were only three long distance telephones and two telex machines, for filing by wire, to accommodate about seventy-five reporters. To operate the telex machines, several well-trained Saudis had been brought in and at first the copy seemed to be moving out at a rapid clip. But late in the evening, as the first deadline for the *Times* was approaching, I noticed the copy was piling up despite an abundance of white-robed men in the filing area. My lead on the Nixon arrival, filed two hours earlier, had not cleared. Ed Finck, the representative of International Telephone and Telegraph, who was making the trip to expedite telex copy, was in deep distress.

"Look," he said. "These guys are good telex operators. They consider it an honor in their country to be here in this job for a visiting President of the United States. So they invited all their relatives down to share the honor and they are so busy visiting no copy is being filed." He said he would try to send the copy for newspapers on deadline through the telex facilities of some of the American companies in Jidda. Finally, three hours after deadline, when I should have been sleeping, I was able to reach my paper by telephone. The telex copy had not arrived. I had to dictate for the second edition.

Ordinarily, Kissinger would have briefed the American press from time to time to provide some insights into what was going on. But he was not briefing, or talking to reporters who tried to draw him out. Presumably, he did not want to be asked embarrassing questions about his performance at Salzburg. When Nixon and Sadat signed an agreement in Cairo, it was released without explanation and some of the first wire service reports indicated that a section of the agreement under which the United States would provide atomic energy to Egypt for peaceful uses, could mean that Egypt, as India had done, might be able to develop an atomic bomb from that aid. For two days, the American officials were kept busy issuing denials.

In Jerusalem, toward the end of the trip, Kissinger finally held a press conference, but by then the curiosity of most of the reporters had been decimated by weariness and diarrhea that went through the Presidential entourage faster than medics could hand out pills. I finally decided that there was less happening than met the eye. What met the eye was ticked off by Ziegler on the way back: 14,775 miles traveled; thirty-one hours in the air; conferences lasting fifty hours and thirty minutes between Nixon and foreign leaders; three Nixon arrival speeches; six official toasts; one press conference (Nixon and Sadat aboard a rolling train in which little was asked and little revealed); the signing of four joint statements, with Egypt, Syria, Jordan, and Israel; and, of course, the symbolic value of an American President visiting the countries involved. I have read nothing since to indicate that anything of great significance was negotiated in the private meetings, as White House officials implied.

It was a classic case of the Presidency controlling, by use of its extraordinary powers, the news written about it. We were so much prisoners of the caravan that we did not know that in Salzburg Nixon suffered an attack of phlebitis and refused orders by his doctors to curtail his activities. If it had happened in Washington, it probably would have leaked out as it did upon Nixon's return from the trip, but in the cocoon that makes up the traveling White House, there is little leaking between compartments. What is covered, how the reporters spend their time, which ones serve on pools, and the information to be distributed, is all decided by the White House, which, in this case, made sure the press was consumed by travel and ceremony. There was not even an opportunity to ask questions that had been accumulating on Watergate. The President's domestic problems had been pre-empted by a foreign trip designed to show an irate nation that it should think twice before dismissing a President who could command so much attention and respect in one of the prime trouble spots of the world.

Nixon was in the United States only five days after the Middle East trip before he departed for Russia and his third annual summit meeting with Leonid Brezhnev, the Soviet leader. There was speculation not discouraged by official sources, that in the meetings in Moscow Nixon might pull off some important agreement, probably in the area of strategic arms limitations, and probably with the willing cooperation of Brezhnev, who was reputed to have a liking and respect for the American President. The Soviet leader found the Watergate charges frivolous under Soviet standards and preferred dealing with Nixon over the unknown quantity of Vice President Ford. By this time, however, I had become so accustomed to trusting my instincts and impressions over words and statements that might emanate from official sources that I tended to discount this speculation. My impressions told me that Nixon, at this stage, was going through the motions of world diplomacy without much hope of making important break-throughs. I had developed what I called my reverse iceberg theory: what you could see on the surface of the policies and substance of the Nixon White House was about all there was.

Enroute to Moscow, Nixon stopped at Brussels to confer again with European leaders and to participate in the signing of a new declaration of principles for the North Atlantic Treaty Organization. One of the questions at Brussels was whether Nixon's newly disclosed phlebitis posed a threat to his life. Although most cases of phlebitis are mild and uncomplicated, sometimes blood clots associated with the ailment can break off in the leg and lodge in the lungs, causing death. Long airplane flights, according to medical experts, can contribute to this danger. Ziegler, who had restricted Dr. Tkach's freedom to talk to reporters about the ailment, spoke for the doctor, quoting him as saying that although Nixon's left leg continued to be swollen, he was no longer suffering pain and that there was "no further possibility of the clotting portion of the difficulty breaking loose." More reassuring than Ziegler's words was the fact that Nixon again took to the streets, as he had in Paris, mingled with the crowds and showed no sign of disability. But in the many hours that I had watched Nixon in the Middle East, at times goose-stepping [English style] with the Arab kings, I had never detected anything wrong. With Nixon, a reporter always had to be suspicious, never surprised by any attempt to conceal developments, whether large or small, and that was why so many hours were wasted in torturous cross-examination of any official who was willing to be cross-examined.

The crowds in Russia who turned out to see the American President were very different from those he had encountered either in Europe or the Middle East. They lined the streets for miles, but they were quiet and reserved, staring at the visiting dignitary more out of curiosity than approval and leaving the impression with American reporters that they were told to be there. It had been the same two years earlier. Reporters who had covered the 1972 summit in Moscow said a striking change in the city was that now there were far more automobiles on the streets. Otherwise it was much the same, including the press room at the Intourist Hotel, which was much too small for the swarms of Soviet and foreign journalists, but had a bar that sold vodka, cold cuts, and a bitter but refreshing orange juice twenty-four hours a day, and there was always babble and confusion.

Détente had been underway for two years, and while the hotels were filled with American businessmen and tourists and the official statements flowing from the summit were friendly and optimistic of close relations in the future, there was always some incident to mar any feeling that détente was taking hold. The American reporters were charged $102 a night for a spartan hotel room (with breakfast) that one might expect to find in a YMCA in the 1930s, a rip-off that American officials were powerless to prevent. A small matter. More disturbing was a lecture I received from one of the Soviet journalists, a man who held a position of some responsibility. In the gravest of tones, he told me that *The New York Times'* Washington bureau was irresponsible in the way it had played up Watergate and attacked Nixon. I might as well have been listening to Al Haig: tenuous and delicate efforts to build a peaceful order in the world were being threatened by a mischievous and petty press.

Hedrick Smith, the *Times'* Moscow bureau chief who had won a Pulitzer Prize for his coverage of the Soviet Union, introduced me to the difficult task that American journalists there face in reporting the news of the Soviet dissidents without offending the authorities to the point of being expelled from the country. It was a situation that required both hard work and courage and, for the most part, American journalists did a remarkable job under trying conditions. When the American television networks covering Nixon sought to report the protests of Soviet citizens—as Smith and his colleagues had been doing on a regular basis—the Soviets pulled the plug and would not allow the broadcasts to go out. The White House put out a mild statement in response to protests from the American journalists saying the American government did not approve of such tactics. But no one in the Nixon White House, either in Washington or Moscow, ever left the impression of being much offended by violations of civil liberties. Interference with internal affairs of another country, Kissinger said many times over, was outside the purview of the United States in the pursuit of its big-power diplomacy. This was understandable. The point here, however, was that the historic American sensitivity to individual freedom seemed lacking in the Nixon government, making overt Soviet oppression seem even more disturbing.

Nixon had other things on his mind. For one, he wanted to tie détente to the personal relationship that existed between him and Brezhnev. In an exchange of toasts at a state dinner on June 27, Nixon said that past agreements between the Soviet Union and the United States "were possible because of a personal relationship that was established between the general secretary and the President of the United States. And that personal relationship extends to the top officials in both of our governments. It has been said that the agreement is only as good as the will of the parties to keep it. Because of our personal relationship, there is no question about our will to keep these agreements and to make more where they are in our mutual interests." This was a little too much, even for Brezhnev, who in a subsequent toast on July 2, seemed to shy away from the highly personalized approach of Nixon. "We wish you and the entire administration and the Congress of the United States every success in giving effect to the good initiatives of peace," he said.

The summit would not settle back into quiet diplomacy and an opportunity for reporters to dig for substance. Movement

and imagery took over again when Nixon and Brezhnev moved
their talks to Yalta, a vacation spot on the Black Sea which
retained the flavor of its Czarist developers despite the hoards
of citizens from the farms and factories who made the beaches
a solid expanse of human flesh. Nixon and Ford conferred for
four hours and twenty-five minutes at Brezhnev's *dacha* on
June 30. Afterwards, one high American official in a private and
off-the-record conversation with a few reporters held out hope
for an important break-through on strategic arms limitation.
But, once again, I felt more secure with my impressions than
with the statements of any official, and my impression was that
not much was happening. It was at Yalta that the limits of the
1974 summit were tentatively decided. And this was why, I later
thought, Nixon's visit to Minsk the next day was of deep personal significance to him.

When we left Yalta early in the morning, it promised to be
a day of empty ceremony and discomfort. The American press
was required to fly on Soviet jets, which must hold the world
record for crowding the maximum number of seats into the
fuselage. When we all squeezed in with baggage, cameras, and
recording equipment, a miracle of compact packing had been
accomplished. Enroute from Simferopol airport—which we
had reached by a hair-raising ride over mountainous roads from
Yalta—to Minsk, one of the four jet engines failed, causing the
plane to lurch sharply to the left. We could only sit in quiet
terror, crowded against each other, as the Soviet pilot brought
the plane under control. For the rest of the trip, there was an
enormous demand for the brown vodka the stewardesses dispensed in small glasses and that pleasantly burned the innards.

Minsk seemed an appropriate city for an American President on a peace mission to visit. Located between Moscow and
Warsaw, Minsk is an industrial city of about one million people
that for centuries has been overrun by invading armies from
the East and West. In World War II it was destroyed by the
Nazis. When Nixon arrived it was celebrating its recapture by
the Soviet armies thirty years earlier, and the wide streets and

heavy buildings and statutary were decorated with red banners and communist slogans.

Nixon went through a day of what seemed to me rather empty ceremonies of speeches and wreath-laying. But as evening approached, he went to the Khatyn Memorial, a few miles outside Minsk, which is at the site of the former village of Kyatyn. On March 22, 1943, according to Soviet historians, the Nazis herded all 149 people of the village, including the elderly and children, into a barn, closed its doors, and set the building afire. When the people managed to break open a door, the invaders machine gunned them. Only three—a man and two children—survived by escaping to a neighboring village.

Nixon, accompanied by Mrs. Nixon, stood before a statue of Joseph Kaminsky, the adult survivor, who was depicted as an emaciated old man holding a dying son. They stopped at the "Wall of Sorrows," which commemorates the victims of concentration camps, and at rows of naked chimneys, each of which represented a destroyed house. "This is very moving," Nixon said as he lingered much longer than scheduled, or needed, to record the visit for television viewers back home. At a tiny pond where visitors traditionally left coins, he and Mrs. Nixon threw in several, saying, "To life." Later, he sat for a long time at a desk which held a guest book. Finally, he wrote, "May this moving memorial to the victims of war reinforce the determination of all those who come here to build a living monument to those who died—a world of peace for their children and their grandchildren. Richard Nixon, President of the United States, July 1, 1974." When they left it was growing dark.

It was just an impression, but I thought the visit to the Khatyn Memorial was a watershed in Nixon's mind during the most important crisis of his life. Whatever is to be said about his Presidency, he did take the long view of history and that had an effect on everything he did. Minsk and the many generations of people who had lived in that crossroads between East and West had been the victims of more wars than anyone cared to remember. Richard Nixon, in his own mind, was trying to bring a new world order that would end the slaughter that seemed to take place at least every generation, and to bring a permanence to the shaky peace that had existed over most of the world since the last great holocaust three decades earlier. In view of this, it was unimportant, trifling really, that the civil liberties of some few people had been violated by his associates, that some laws had been broken in his efforts to establish a order of peace. And after five and one-half years in the Presidency of the United States, he was not impressed by arguments that his initiatives could be continued by other men. This was his unique contribution that was now threatened by partisan efforts back home to remove him. The Moscow summit would not produce any break-through sufficient to demonstrate his indispensibility. It only kept détente on the track laid down in 1972. Two days later, he returned to the United States from his last foreign trip as President. The fact that he had controlled the news to his favor for almost a month was not sufficient to offset the growing mass of evidence against him.

12
THE WEEK THAT WAS

It would have seemed less apocalyptic had it not been for the kids on the streets. In early August 1974, a gray haze—a mixture of humidity and pollution—hung over Washington. The civil servants, lawyers, consultants, and lobbyists who work in the buildings for blocks around the White House, swarmed onto the streets in staggered arrivals, over long lunch periods, and during struggled departures. Their most immediate and urgent goal was to reach the next air-conditioned compound. Yet the tattered kids would stand all day trying for the attention of those who rushed by. They wanted to talk and to paper the crowd with pamphlets announcing:

JESUS
FESTIVAL

Jesus Folk/Rock Music
along with Bible Rap

Washington Monument
N.W. Quadrant

Sponsored by God the Father & Co.

But few would listen or take their papers. For a decade ragtag armies of youth had been decending on the nation's capital, in one way or another concerned about wayward mankind. First, there were the civil rights marches in which they displayed an idealistic, naïve faith in national leaders and institutions; their method was petition of grievances and their goal reform. Then came the long and fruitless marches against the war in Vietnam; slowly they became embittered and violent, until in May 1971, they fought their last big battle with the authorities; crushed by mass arrests, tear gas and billy clubs, they had retreated in disorder and shame. Now the hated Presidency of Richard Milhous Nixon was falling, by the dead weight of its own corruption, and the only radical kids around were Jesus Freaks, many of whom had been the full route, from protest to violence to drugs and to the monumental turn-off, until now they were involved in a religious movement so primitive that it had no room for politics or social justice. And to the other veterans of the youth wars not so saved, it made little difference that Nixon was tottering; the succeeding government would be fatally flawed, also. That was the way it was, so that coming to Washington for protest or celebration was a childish thing of the past. The Nixon Presidency would have to be buried by the establishment.

"The Week That Was," as it became known in the White House press room, began with some ominous signs of more trouble for the President but no indication of an imminent resignation. In July, the Supreme Court, finally becoming a party to the Watergate case, ruled that Nixon must turn over to the special prosecutor additional tapes and documents sought for prosecution of the Watergate defendants. The President received the news in San Clemente, after the House Judiciary Committee had voted to recommend impeachment and as the full House was preparing to take up the question in mid-August, with prospects of an anti-Nixon vote virtually certain and growing. Yet nothing seemed any different within the small group around Nixon. While the House Judiciary Committee had displayed to the nation by television that it was a remarkably astute and judicious body, more so than anyone famil-

iar with the House of Representatives had expected, Ron Ziegler had said on behalf of the President that it was a kangaroo
court. The news from the Supreme Court was received with
regret but the President's assistants said it was yet another blow
from which the Nixon presidency would recover. It seemed to
me that the White House people still were viewing the conflict
through the same distorted lenses that had marred their perception of reality in the past.

On Sunday, August 4, I was enjoying a day at home when
William M. Blair of our Washington bureau called to say the
President had hurriedly summoned his aides to Camp David,
where he was spending the weekend after returning from San
Clemente. A quick check showed there was no sign of a national
or international crisis. It had to be about Watergate and most
probably the tapes the President would have to release in the
next few days. I was able to piece together from some low-level
White House officials enough information to indicate Nixon was
considering releasing some of the tapes to the public before
submitting them to authorities Yet the exercise was conducted
with secrecy that would have rivaled that of the Cuban missile
crisis or the bombing of Cambodia. Here was an administration
in deep trouble, needing all the help it could summon in order
to survive, yet it still dealt with the press in the most supercilli-
ous way. However deep Richard Nixon's troubles, he never
bent in his resolve to hold the press in contempt. Previous
administrations, I thought, would have had background sessions
or at least perfunctory question and answer periods for the
reporters who were swarming onto the White House for information. Instead, the Ziegler press office merely confirmed that
meetings were held between Nixon and his aides.

The disclosures of the next day were more damaging to
Nixon than anyone on the outside had expected. He first issued
a statement saying he was releasing the transcripts of three
conversations of June 23, 1973, which he conceded would further damage his fight against impeachment. In the statement
he admitted that the evidence showed that six days after the

Watergate burglary he ordered a halt to the investigation of the
break-in for political, as well as national security reasons, and
that he kept the evidence from his lawyers and supporters on
the House Judiciary Committee. His previous statements that
the tapes he had released in the spring told the full story of
Watergate were exposed as a lie. Probably any other President
would have resigned then and there. But Nixon went on trying
to control events. He released his statement several hours
before the transcripts were made available, thus putting his
own interpretation on the conversations before the White
House press could draw its own conclusions. James St. Clair, the
story went, discovered the damning evidence in the course of
preparing the tapes for release to the courts. What a smart man
St. Clair had been! In press conferences he had held during
"Cocktails with Clawson" he had insisted over and over that he
did not know the contents of the tapes under subpoena. He
would have become so involved in detail, he said, that he could
never perform his primary function of defending the President
in Congress and in the courts.

✗ Nixon's resolve to stay on despite the damning evidence
was more than the President's extraordinary persistence, which
had become second nature to him in a long career of political
fighting and hanging on by his fingernails. There was an institutional refusal to give in, to accept reality even when staunch
Nixon supporters in Congress, such as Representative Charles
E. Wiggins of California and Senator Robert Dole of Kansas,
were abandoning the Nixon cause. This was seen in the strange
cabinet meeting of Tuesday, August 6. According the reports
pieced together later, the members assembled around the oval
table in the Cabinet Room, looking as if nothing unusual were
happening. Nixon, appearing grave but calm, said he wanted to
open the meeting with a discussion of a subject uppermost on
every one's mind, inflation. But first he talked of his own resolve
to stay in office as the impeachment process ran its course.
When everyone emerged from the meeting ninety minutes
later, those participants who would answer questions asked

what all the fuss was about, asserting that they were solely concerned with running the country. "Let's not have this tragedy obscure the fact that we have a lot of determined people at work," said Treasury Secretary William E. Simon, as a throng of reporters and photographers followed him out the White House gate and down Pennsylvania Avenue.

But the next day it was clear, even to people in the White House, that Nixon not only could not win in the House, he could not count on more than a handful of senators to vote against his conviction. Previously, he had hoped to hold the support of the thirty-four senators, mostly southern Democrats and western Republicans, but one by one, they were publicly or privately leaving the reservation. Word leaked out that Alexander Haig, with the help of Kissinger, was advising Nixon to resign. Late that afternoon, Wednesday, August 7, Nixon called in three Republican leaders who had helped him in the past—Senator Hugh Scott of Pennsylvania, Senator Barry Goldwater of Arizona, and Representative John J. Rhodes of Arizona—to ask their assessment of the situation. Nixon had his feet propped on his desk in the Oval Office throughout the thirty-minute meeting, they said later, while they told him the situation was grave indeed.

The last two days were like a river rushing to become a waterfall. Out of all the confusion and suspense it is the little things I remember best: the expression of pained determination on Rabbi Korff's round face as he emerged from the Executive Office Building with Bruce Hershensohn after a meeting with Nixon, and marched forth to mobilize his intense army of press haters, who succeeded in jamming the White House switchboard with calls urging the President not to resign; cameramen and photographers descending on the White House press room in such unprecedented numbers that the air conditioning would not accommodate the heat of the bodies and the lights, and the windows had to be opened to the sultry August air; the sight of Jerry Warren conducting briefings in the same laconic manner he always had, as if nothing really had changed;

the reports of the pathetic meetings between Nixon and his family, who along with Rabbi Korff, were about the only ones urging him to stay and fight; the crowds along Pennsylvania Avenue staring through the cast iron fence as White House aides and journalists rushed about, and as Nixon himself occasionally could be seen moving between the Executive Office Building and the West Wing of the White House.

On Thursday, it became known that Nixon would go on television that night and announce that he would resign. The official announcement said only that he would make a television appearance. Word of the resignation came privately from Haig and others. But by this time I had become so distrustful of anything said by anyone on the Nixon staff that I would not give my editors iron-clad assurance that there would be a resignation. This was a very important matter to the *Times*. For several months, as was the case with most major newspapers, we had accumulated a number of stories for use should a Presidential resignation occur. The television appearance was scheduled for 8:30 P.M. (Until the very last the preoccupation with imagery over substance guided the Nixon people to seek prime television time.), after our first edition deadline, which would have to be stretched for the occasion. In retrospect, my distrust of the advance notice of the resignation was not realistic. The truth was I had been infected by the siege mentality I was assigned to cover. I could see Nixon at the last minute pulling a trick on his old enemy, the eastern establishment press.

A. M. Rosenthal, the *Times'* managing editor, decided to go ahead with what had come to be known on the paper as the "quit package" of stories, but to remain flexible enough to throw it all out at the last minute should the resignation not materialize. I had to write a dummy lead with blanks to be filled in with details from the broadcast, but we did not move it to New York until we heard the news from the President's lips. This, then, was how the lead story of the historic edition of August 9 began:

WASHINGTON, Aug. 8—Richard Milhous Nixon, the 37th President of the United States, announced tonight that he had given up his long and arduous fight to remain in office and would resign, effective at noon tomorrow.

Gerald Rudolph Ford, whom Mr. Nixon nominated for Vice President last October 12, will be sworn tomorrow at the same hour as the 38th President, to serve out the 895 days remaining in Mr. Nixon's second term.

The bigger the news, the easier it is to write. With major events, a flat, full statement of facts is better than clever writing, because the facts carry the story. Any good rewrite person in the country could have written that lead story. The difficult problem of trying to explain, within the boundaries of traditional journalism, Nixon and his court while still in power was over.

The day we had long awaited had finally arrived, but I do not think anyone expected the feeling of relief that swept through Washington. The issue seemed to be resolved to the satisfaction of almost everyone outside the Nixon circle. It was the certainty of impeachment and conviction that effected the resignation. The constitutional process for removing a President had worked—without the long and painful agony of a Senate trial. Many Nixon supporters who had stood by him until the final week were at last convinced that the Watergate issue was one of significance that should have been pursued. I no longer got mail from my antagonists, except for one or two letters expressing disappointment in Nixon. Rabbi Korff's army folded its tent and silently crept away, at least for the time being. The liberals who had advocated impeachment in 1973, before it became respectable, were vindicated. Official Washington proclaimed, with some surprise, that the system worked. Gerald Ford was such a contrast to his predecessor, with his plainness and open manner and the assurance of his acceptance speech that "here the people rule," that relief gave way to euphoria. The White House press felt it especially when Jerry ter Horst, known to his colleagues as an able and honest Washington journalist, was named to succeed Ziegler.

On Saturday, I wrote a long story for the Sunday *Times* "Week in Review" section summarizing the Watergate saga and the news of the past few days and, early in the evening, fell into a deep sleep. When I awoke on Sunday, the humidity and haze had gone and it was a clear, cool, sparkling day—the kind that rarely occurs in Washington in August. In the afternoon, my wife, Betty, and our daughters, Mary, Anne, and Jill, drove to Sugarloaf Mountain, an outcropping of granite in nearby Maryland that provides a hiking area of trees, rocks, and ferns. At the top of the mountain we found wild blackberries growing in the thickets. As I popped berries into a handkerchief and gleefully watched the white cloth turn purple, the events of the past year and a half rushed through my head, and I could not block them out.

In many ways, it had been the strangest of periods, an aberration from the broad sweep of the American political experience, not so much in what had occurred, as in the attitudes of those in high office in the closing months. Not a single person who held a responsible job in the Nixon White House had resigned in a public expression of indignation, despite the fact that it had been patently clear for many months before the end that the sleaziest kind of dishonesty and deception was underway. On the contrary, there had never been any sign that the men and women who served Richard Nixon were at all offended by what went on. If there was shock I was not able to detect it. There was dismay, but only at the fact that the administration was in deep trouble. The norm was to defend Nixon just as if they were defending a respectable political position in Washington's ever-present struggle for party supremacy. Even Anne Armstrong, counselor to the President, and whom I had held in high regard, ultimately joined the Rabbi Korff group in publicly berating the press for stirring up trouble and unfairly attacking the President. Yet those in the White House, after Haldeman and Ehrlichman left, never seemed to me as different from the norm as they were frequently depicted. Their view of public morals was not unlike that of the rest of us. As a group, I thought, they were not an unrepresentative sample of the American educated class.

But more was involved than amoral attitudes, self-serving motives, or the strange sense of personal loyalty that some seemed to hold for Nixon. There was something about the powers and mystique of the office surrounding the man who occupied it that raised the tolerance level of those who served there. To them, the President of the United States, could not be held to the same standards as others. The office was *his* by mandate of the people to do what he wanted for four years. This belief had grown deep in Washington and was not easily diminished. A disturbing question flowed from this thought: Would I or any of my colleagues have done any different if we were accidently thrown into a high White House office at the peak of the Nixon powers? I prefer to think so, but I cannot be sure, so strong are the influences that turn people's heads once they become part of the White House compound.

What of General Haig and Dr. Kissinger? Would they emerge as heros for having successfully urged the President to resign, but only after Nixon had lost his support in Congress and could not possibly survive an impeachment trial? I cannot not make a judgment on Kissinger. He was, during most of the Watergate period, so engaged in running the State Department and foreign policy that, as far as I knew, he was not involved in the White House intrigues on Watergate. Haig, however, was so deeply involved that he became a case study in how the office separates men from their better judgments. Haig's level of tolerance for corruption was high indeed. It was he who said "some sinister force" must have made the eighteen and one half-minute gap in a crucial tape. The sinister force was never identified. Some in the special prosecutor's office thought Nixon himself must have performed the erasure. Yet as far as anyone from the press room could determine, Haig never made any supreme effort to find out. It was Haig who appeared to be instrumental in politicizing the Nixon lawyers, even as he himself had become politicized. One weekend in Key Biscayne, in the spring of 1974, Haig had gone into a rage over what he thought was unfair newspaper coverage of Watergate, and had St. Clair flown down to put out a denial statement that was not part of the legal defense. He had supported Nixon in every conceivable way, even as the stench of corruption was all about.

There had been reports that in the latter days Nixon had showed increased signs of instability and there were fears among the White House staff that he would become irrational. But there was no reliable way to learn the truth. Those around Nixon seemed incapable of telling a reporter what was true but perfectly capable of giving self-serving evidence. From what I was able to discern from those on the outside and from what I saw and heard, Nixon's behavior in the closing days seemed fully consistent with what we had been witnessing for a year and a half. That he was able to function at all was remarkable, yet he hung on until that final tearful goodbye in the East Room on the morning of his resignation, when he evoked the memory of his dead mother. If Nixon was unstable, it was an instability that had been there all along. Haig, it was said, had, in effect, acted as President as Nixon increasingly faltered in that role. But it had been a staff-run Presidency for a long time. Kissinger ran foreign policy, and Nixon had delegated domestic policy to the Office of Management and Budget and certain assistants.

Even at the end, when many were looking for subterranean plots and meanings, I suspected that the reverse iceberg theory was still applicable—there was not much more there than we could see. I yearned for a transcript of Haig and Kissinger telling Nixon he had to go, but by then the behavior of the cast of characters was so predictable I believed that almost any member of the White House press could have written it off the wall.

And what of Nixon himself? After a year and a half of thinking and puzzling about the man, his actions and his motives, I could not explain him, either to myself or to anyone else.

I understood that his behavior was usually predictable. Virtually everything he did up to his last days in office was consistent with what he and others had revealed about his earlier life and his approach to politics. Without understanding why, I could not escape the thought that Nixon, perhaps unconsciously, had a death wish. I could not imagine Lyndon Johnson, or any other President, not destroying the tapes before it was discovered that they existed. Nixon knew early in 1973 that he was in deep trouble in Watergate. It was not until midsummer that the Ervin committee learned Presidential conversations had been recorded. Nixon was under no obligation to make the tapes; he was under no obligation to keep them, until Congress and the prosecutors took legal steps to obtain them. Certainly Nixon must have felt so confident in his ability to maintain executive privilege that he did not think other branches of government could ever lay their hands on them. But other evidence suggested that overconfidence in the powers of his office was not the only reason he did not have the tapes destroyed.

A good case could be made from his actions thereafter that he set himself up to be caught in the Watergate case. In the spring of 1973, while prosecutors were hot on the trail of a White House cover-up, Nixon, or someone under his jurisdiction, had a segment of a crucial tape erased in such a clumsy way that it was clear to prosecutors that a conversation concerned with how to deal with the Watergate crime purposely had been cut out of the recording. Every disclosure Nixon made about his taxes and personal financing was done in a way that invited suspicions and led to the uncovering of further damaging information. A long succession of such actions led me to accept the death-wish theory. I could not imagine any public official with a desire to prevail leaving such a trail of damning evidence.

Every thought turned up another irony. Nixon, who hated the press and sought to deny it information at every turn, provided the best story Washington reporters had the opportunity to cover in many years. The Watergate story and the fall of the

President had every element that makes journalism exciting—suspense and mystery about people in high places. Yet it went beyond that. Nixon changed the course of journalism, though not in the way he had planned. For a period of almost two years, Washington journalists were so preoccupied with the Watergate story that enormous areas of the government once watched closely by hosts of reporters went virtually uncovered. We no longer knew what went on in many of the departments and agencies. The government programs that had been enacted in recent years—their worth as yet unproven—did not have the scrutiny they would have had in an administration in which performance of the government, rather than intrigues and lawbreaking, was the focus of attention.

In a sense, this served the Nixon Presidency, because, basically, the Nixon people did not want government domestic programs handled on the national level. They wanted to return whatever authority they could to the state and local levels, to undo the work of Democratic administrations of recent decades. For five and one-half years, Nixon and the high officials of his administration traveled the country making speeches in which they berated the federal bureaucracy and the programs of which they themselves were in charge. This theme predominated in Nixon domestic policy. Yet here, too, there was a measure of fraud. While proclaiming the need for a reduction of federal involvement, which was carried out in education, health, research, manpower training, and antipoverty programs, among others, the Nixon administration, out of a desire to capture a larger political constituency, increased in concert with Congress federal involvement on another level. This included the regulatory powers of the federal government in the areas of environmental protection, product safety, transportation, and consumer interests. Yet we, the media, had never properly sorted it out and measured it, because we were too busy with the big suspense story. And as a result, there did not seem to be much public awareness of what was phony and what was substantive in the government's performance under Nixon.

One of the sins of Washington reporting had long been that we were too much inclined to chase the easy story, the topic of current popularity, without ever coming to grips with the hidden though powerful forces that have an impact on people's lives. For years, those in authority in Washington journalism had paid lip service, for example, to covering the regulatory agencies in a systematic and thorough way, to discover how the public interest was being sacrificed. But not many news organizations had ever really done it, because few reporters wanted to perform the drudgery needed to accomplish the job; and editors, in their endless demand for copy, did not want to let reporters invest the time that might be needed to dig out important material. There were quicker rewards, say, in analyzing the President's mood, in describing the way the way the administration lobbyists performed on Capitol Hill or in speculating about the next Presidential candidate. However, Washington journalism was, I thought, in the process of maturing--a process in which a number of the news organizations had begun setting their own priorities on what they thought was important for the public interest and in investing time and talent in those areas --when the Watergate story burst upon the scene.

Watergate was an issue so basic to the survival of democratic government that it had to be reported in detail and followed diligently, so much so that it was all-consuming. The maturing process that was underway in reporting of government performance simply stopped when the Watergate story drained off talent, resources, and time. Moreover, the Washington journalists long concerned with government performance found themselves in another and more exciting league. Now it was over. Clearly an era had passed, and I had serious doubts that many in journalism would be willing to go back to the hard work required for thorough reporting of government performance. The newspapers, it had often been said, found themselves admirably equipped to fight the last war but never the current one. Would the media now spend its resources on a search for crooks and wrongdoing when the times might call for another kind of search? If not, what kind of reporting should emerge in the post-Watergate era?

As for myself, I could not see how I could ever again be intellectually excited, as I once was, by what went on in the Office of Management and Budget or the Department of Health, Education and Welfare. Furthermore, I was filled with dread, rather than relief, at the thought of White House reporting returning to the norm, with the President and other officials making themselves open to reporters, but only so far as to use the media for their own purposes, and not to publish the truth. Somehow it seemed that the truth had been served better in the period of confrontation, when reporters had to rely on their perceptions and impressions, than in the previous years of Nixon, Johnson, and Kennedy, when the White House used the media as a force to be manipulated rather than allowed to function in its own way as a conveyor of reality.

A conveyor of reality. Perhaps we took our responsibilities too seriously. I did not know. The blackberry picking was over. Half way down the mountain we stopped to rest. In the late afternoon, rays of sunlight through the leaves were almost horizontal. I lay on a log face down and thought about being a reporter. The trouble with being a reporter is that you are judged not on what you might have done in the past, but what you did today. I had known reporters who performed magnificently for twenty years, but when they went into a slump for a year or so everyone forgot their past record as young challengers came along to take their place. Novelists, historians, poets, and other writers could delay writing until their creativity returned. Editors could concern themselves with various subjects and not display to the world the limits of their ability. But the daily reporter was constantly being put to the test, without even the time to renew himself. I knew that in a week or so of filing my story of Nixon's fall, the facts would be history to newspaper editors and readers, and I would be judged anew on how well I could convey the reality of a new administration with new people and new circumstances, and I did not know whether I could succeed.

These thoughts, however, could not suppress the aura of good feeling that swept over us all that day. The forces that threatened American democracy had been defeated. The press, the judicial, and legislative branches had functioned as the founding fathers seemed to have intended. The government of the United States had been renewed. There was new hope for future generations. All around me were fallen trees of decades past, decaying and becoming part of the sparse soil that sustained the forest. Out of them grew mountain laurel, new oaks and flowering vines. In such a place, I thought, a person who had been a part of the great conflicts of our age could die without trauma or regret.

13
A BRIEF HONEYMOON

The beginning of the Ford administration was a confused, hectic time for all concerned, but it was apparent early on that the months ahead would be a period of testing—to determine what the post-Watergate Presidency would be under people of restraint and sensitivity to the public will and to see how the White House press would function under more normal conditions after having gone through an ordeal and transformation. My hope was that neither would be the same; that the hard lessons of the past would result in a Presidency reduced in staff, royal trappings, and self-importance, so that it might better function in both leadership and exercise of authority under a democratic system; and in a press that would remain independent, aloof from the blandishments of the institution and determined to sort out the hokum from the substance.

At first, almost everything seemed drastically changed. The new press secretary, Jerry ter Horst, who had been chief of the *Detroit News* Washington bureau, was at once believable, not only because he was one of us, but because he was a rare individual whose sense of integrity commanded belief, a quality I had never seen within a President's staff. Ford brought with him to the Presidency a group of plain people, men like John O. Marsh, a conservative Democrat from Virginia who had served in Congress, and Philip Buchen, Ford's long-time friend from Grand Rapids, whose talk and appearance was that of a small-town lawyer. Quite suddenly, the White House seemed to be a place of openness and candor. This was noticeable all down the line, even to the police on the guard posts who appeared relieved and happy at having superiors who were not under criminal investigation. Ford made a point of inviting people to the White House whom the Nixon people had avoided—liberal democrats, moderate Republicans, even the eastern press. My wife, Betty, and I were invited to Ford's first state dinner, for King Hussein of Jordan. For almost two years I had felt like I was entering enemy territory whenever I passed into the White House compound. Now we were being escorted through the great halls and having our names announced by loud-speaker in the East Room. Never mind my objections to the press becoming too cozy with officialdom. It was a time for celebration, and everyone stayed very late, dancing out the deadness of the past.

The press room seemed a much healthier place, both on the part of the press office staff and the journalists. The White House press had an infusion of new blood, largely the reporters who had been covering Ford and who were merged with the White House regulars for the transition. The Ford press brought a new perspective of the President. For many months they had been following the Vice President on his extensive travels throughout the country, suffering through long days and nights of dreary dinners, receptions, and rallies. Reporters such as Majorie Hunter of the *Times* had gained insights into Jerry Ford and made valuable contacts on his staff. There were so many people in the press room to report on the new administration that it continued for some time to be the sweaty, confused scene it was in the last days of the Nixon administration. Yet all of this was a welcome change. By this time we were so accustomed to strange occurrences that no one seemed impressed by one of the strangest of all: the Gerald Rudolph Ford Washington had known for so long as a somewhat dull and plodding minority leader, was now a celebrated President, praised by those who had never found much merit in him in the past.

It seemed a long time since the previous October when Ford's metamorphosis began. I was sitting at my desk in the *Times* bureau one afternoon after Agnew resigned, typing a story, when Clifton Daniel emerged from his office and told me, "Jerry Ford is one of those being considered for Vice President." I had heard Ford's name mentioned for the position, but I thought he was being promoted by his friends on Capitol Hill simply as a matter of courtesy, that his chances of being nominated were nil. "Jerry isn't qualified to become President," I said. "I know," Clifton replied, "but he's one of those at the top of the list, nevertheless."

Even though Nixon was then clinging tenaciously to office, many in Washington believed that whoever he picked for Vice President most likely would succeed him in the Presidency. It took me some time to become accustomed to the thought of Gerald R. Ford as President. I had known him in the mid-1960s, when I was covering Congress and he was the popular leader of a small and ineffectual minority party in the House. Perhaps I was too much influenced by the prevailing view of Ford in the House press gallery: the view that Jerry Ford was a nice guy but was so mired in the sterile political philosophy of the bulk of congressional Republicans that he was both totally predictable and without an original idea of his own. Year after year, the major contribution of Ford and the minority bloc, I thought, had been to oppose, unselectively, the expansive domestic programs and legislation of the Democratic majority while supporting, too uncritically, some aspects of the foreign policy of Democratic Presidents.

Ford's ambition was to be speaker, a position he would have easily assumed had the Republicans ever gained a majority while he was the House minority leader. For years, he traveled the country speaking and raising money for Republican House candidates. The biggest break-through for him came in the 1966 elections, when the Republicans gained forty-seven seats in the House. Shortly after the new representatives arrived in Washington early in 1967, Ford and other House GOP leaders took them to a secluded resort near Warrenton, Virginia, for a training session, and invited the press to cover the event. It was not the most newsworthy event I had ever covered, but because Congress was then my beat, I considered it a good opportunity to size up the new Republican members. It was the kind of event that required a reporter to strain for a lead. In one story, I depicted Ford as "clucking over his new brood." As it appeared in the first edition, the result of either a typographical error or a mischievous linotype operator, the story said Ford was "clucking over his new broad." It was my just reward for using such a cliché, but Ford was much amused by the error, which provided comic relief for a sober convention. I was surprised to learn later from Majorie Hunter that in almost every speech as Vice President, Ford had told an embellished version of that story. It had appeared in an obscure position far back in the paper, but the way Ford told it, as warm-up humor, the *Times*, under John Herbers' by-line, had Ford on the front page sporting a new broad.

Over the years, the reporters I knew in Washington developed a genuine affection for Jerry Ford as a person, but were turned off by his approach to issues and government. Journalists are an irreverent bunch who tend to have less faith in private business and institutions than they do in government and the democratic decisions of the unwashed masses, while Republicans of the Ford mold take the opposite approach and are more attracted to convention. In this difference there is a chemistry at work that breeds a certain measure of distrust. Ford, for example, can go to a Rotary Club luncheon and be a true believer, while most of the journalists I know can barely endure the ceremony. Some of us were punished early in our reporting careers by being assigned to cover the back-slapping luncheon meetings of the civic clubs, and we have never gotten over it. It was Ralph McGill, the late editor of the *Atlanta Constitution*, who was credited with saying, "There must be something wrong with grown men who like to stand up and sing dead sober in the middle of the day." When I left Congress in 1968 to cover the national political campaigns, Jerry Ford was, in my mind, the true Rotarian, and I continued to think of him that way in the ensuing years.

As Vice-President, however, Ford displayed qualities that were compelling in the midst of Watergate. The congressional committees that scrutinized his private and public life were unable to find any evidence that he had been a participant in the corruption that had been a part of the Washington scene for so long, even though he had been deeply involved in the collection and dispersal of campaign money, the root of improper influence of public policy. He also showed a remarkably healthy attitude toward public criticism of his actions and policies in view of the fact that the past two Presidents, Nixon and Johnson, had viewed such criticism as improper personal attacks. When Ford became President he showed a kind of grace I had never seen in him before. His performance in Chicago, where he made his first public appearance outside Washington as President, was one example. Suddenly Jerry Ford, the colorless House minority leader, appeared very Presidential, almost charismatic, but without any sign of pomposity, as he waved to admiring crowds as his motorcade moved down Michigan Avenue to the Conrad Hilton Hotel. In his speech before the Veterans of Foreign Wars, he displayed the best of leadership, I thought, by choosing an organization which had steadfastly opposed amnesty as a means of healing the divisions of the country. And he did it with style, conveying a feeling of compassion for the young without any sense of condescension for his audience of old veterans.

Although my first impressions of Ford as President were not to last, the fact that he was able to handle the office as well as he did points up the enormously high expectations that most of us have held for the Presidency. Undoubtedly there are thousands of people in the United States with the ability, background, humility, and understanding of our democratic institutions to make a competent President. Yet, in 1975, Democrats across the country, while holding the Nixon and Ford regimes to be disastrous, were in despair over the seeming lack of a good contender for the 1976 Presidential election. Not until a man becomes President can Americans imagine him as such. In addition to being all-wise on the full range of foreign and domestic policies, the President is expected to be the nation's chief educator, spiritual leader, and symbol of the national spirit enshrined in regal surroundings. This is due in part, I believe, to an accumulation of myths about the Presidency. One is that there is something about the office that makes the occupant become an unselfish leader whose only interest is the welfare of the country and who is not consumed by the passions and jealousies of ordinary men.

In December 1972, my last assignment as urban affairs reporter for the *Times* was to cover a reunion of civil rights leaders with former President Johnson at the University of Texas in Austin. It was a nostalgic occasion, the last meeting between those who had fought the great civil rights campaigns of the 1950s and 1960s and the President who had publicly sided with them before they became disillusioned by his use of resources for the Vietnam War. In Austin, they were in despair over the seeming indifference of the Nixon administration to their cause. Johnson, who had a failing heart and only a few more weeks to live, was barely able to make his way to the podium, yet sought once again to be the great reconciler. All Presidents, he said, so feel the weight of responsibility on assuming office that their chief concern is to do what is right once they know what to do. He suggested that they ask for a meeting with Nixon, who was about to enter a second term, and give him guidance on what was right. Johnson was sincere, which suggested to me that Presidents themselves believe the myths of their office. The evidence of the last few years is that the Presidency is no pinnacle of high motives and altruism. When those who occupy the office believe that it is, mistaken judgments become all the larger.

The Washington press was widely criticized for its glowing, uncritical reports of Ford's first days and weeks as President.

The criticism may have been justified. The contrast between Ford and what had gone before was so great that most of us were somewhat overwhelmed by it. Furthermore, there is a tendency among journalists to exaggerate the story, whatever it is. Overall, however, the major development in the first month of Ford's Presidency was the change in character from the Nixon Presidency. I had long believed that the only honest reporting, the only means of getting at the truth, must be shaped by what the reporter perceives to be the trends and shape of the development or institution he is covering. If this approach to reporting showed the depravity of the Nixon regime, which I believe it did, then the same approach had to point up the positive change under Ford. The fact was that it had been too many years since the United States had a President who did not hold legitimate institutions and competent persons in contempt for opposing what the White House held to be right. Ford's acceptance of dissent, his openness and straight-forward approach to his duties was an accomplishment of major importance to the country. And that was the story of the Ford White House until the demands of the institution and Ford's proclivity for convention took over.

14
THE RETURN TO
NORMALCY

I do not remember the precise time, but it must have been before 8 A.M. Sunday morning, September 7, one month after Nixon resigned, that I was awakened by the telephone. It was the White House press office calling to say there would be an important announcement that morning. The secretary who called would not say what it was about. Probably she did not know. I dressed quickly and drove through the empty Washington streets and entered the White House grounds by the southwest gate. A flock of reporters and photographers, all as sleepy-eyed and as puzzled as I, were gathering for an announcement by ter Horst. While we were waiting, word leaked out and spread like wildfire through the press room: it was a Nixon pardon. The news, as it poured forth all day in a series of briefings, came as a shock, not so much for what was done— Ford had hinted on several occasions that he would grant a pardon, just as he had promised conditional amnesty for draft evaders—as the fact that he did it so quickly and did not demand concessions on the former President's part in return. Like a great divide, the Nixon pardon became the promontory of the early Ford Presidency.

Ford's action set off a flurry of speculation that he and the former President had struck a deal before Nixon left office; that the new President was honoring a commitment he made to the man who put him in line for the Presidency. After the record of Watergate, it was not unreasonable for such a suspicion to arise, but I never subscribed to that explanation. It seemed from the evidence at hand and a knowledge of Ford that a more mundane reason was in order. Ford and Nixon, despite their differences in character, shared pretty much the same constituency and, although they were not close personally, there was a political affinity that transcended the sense of impropriety that many felt was involved in the pardon. Furthermore, in the traditional line of politics to which Ford belonged, one repays one's debts to a colleague. Not only had Ford considered himself an adjunct of Nixon's administration while in Congress, but Nixon had chosen him as Vice President. Above that, it was apparent that Ford viewed the Presidency in the conventional way. Nixon, he said, had suffered enough; he had paid a penalty by giving up the Presidency. In Washington, the conventional way of looking at the Presidency was that it belonged to the man elected to fill it for the prescribed term of office. This was the way Nixon had looked at it—he had a mandate to rule, he kept saying as the Watergate investigations closed in—and it was rare to find anyone who had been part of the Washington scene for long who would hold that the office belonged to the people and the person who defiled it no longer had privileges under it, even though that was what the Constitution said.

Aside from the pardon, which raised the first serious doubts about Ford's motives, it was his conventional view of the Presidency, as well as his approach to policy issues, that set the pattern for his administration in the succeeding months. Before the pardon, Ford was pretty much himself, the plain man from Grand Rapids. The White House bureaucracy, which like all bureaucracies has a life of its own, had not yet superimposed its own mark on the Ford administration. Ford's early speeches, which caught the imagination of many who had doubted Ford's ability for high office, were written by his long-time assistant, Robert T. Hartmann, before Hartmann got ensnared in White House politics and was put in charge of a stable of Presidential speech writers. It was apparent after the first few weeks in office that Ford had no plans for making any major changes in the White House as an institution. Honesty and openness on his own part, Ford said on several occasions, would set an example for those under him. Over a period of months, he put his own people in charge and had a code of ethics drawn up for them to follow. But he accepted without question many of the excesses that had contributed to the White House difficulties of the past: the swollen staff, the propaganda apparatus atuned to perpetuating the myths of the office, the infighting among staff members for authority and closeness to the President, the regal surroundings and pomp. All of this was to have an important bearing on the way in which the press was able to report what went on within the institution.

Ter Horst's departure was symbolic of the bureaucracy and convention taking over. The reason for his resignation, he said, was that he disagreed with the Nixon pardon, but I was later convinced that beyond that he felt he could not function in the forthright way he knew he must as part of the omeiging Presidential court. He was the President's chief public relations adviser, but he was not even consulted about what public reaction to the pardon might be. That in itself was a classic White House phenomenon. Apparently, the President and the few aides he did consult felt themselves wrapped in sufficient wisdom that they did not need the advice of the person in the best position to know. As for the press, the skepticism, even the deep distrust of official acts and explanations, continued as the new administration reached its norm. But in retrospect we were not nearly as independent as we thought ourselves to be. By and large, White House reporting reverted to what it had been before Watergate, I thought, a rather superficial overreporting of the day to day actions of the President and his assistants, while the White House, rather than the reporters, decided the shape of the story.

Before describing how the press functioned of its own volition, however, it may be useful to document some of the ways in which the institution functioned. Immediately after the Nixon pardon, when much of the country was in an uproar over what had been done, ter Horst resigned. As a result, the burden of conducting the White House briefings fell to Jack Hushen, the deputy press secretary, who previously had served as chief public relations officer for the Department of Justice. One of the points of harsh criticism directed against Ford in granting the pardon was that he was letting off scot free the man who had been in charge during Watergate and who, in fact, had accepted the responsibility while his associates were being prosecuted and threatened with long jail sentences. During a news briefing the day after the pardon, Hushen said there was a possibility of the Watergate defendants being pardoned, too. This brought a series of anxious questions. Who authorized Hushen to make such a statement? He could not say. Peter Lisagor of the *Chicago Daily News*, a salty veteran of the White House press corps, asked Hushen if he knew what he was saying, if he knew that his statement would be interpreted to mean that Ford was considering pardons for Haldeman, Ehrlichman, Mitchell, and the others. Hushen stuck by his statement in its murky form during the long and stormy briefing.

I could not believe that the President wanted such a statement to stand. Before I completed my story late in the afternoon, I called Hushen and asked him if he would like to change the statement or amplify it. He said no, and there was no off-the-record guidance or explanation that a Washington reporter expects when such a sensitive subject is involved. I later learned from several sources how the statement originated. At a meeting of the President's aides, the enormous amount of criticism of the pardon was the center of discussion. Even the calls and telegrams pouring into the White House were heavily against the pardon, some angry in tone. In an effort to allay the angry reaction, someone on the staff thought it might be helpful to say that at least some consideration was being given to pardoning the Watergate defendants at some point in the prosecution process. Hushen was instructed—I was never able to find out by whom—to say what he did, but to go no further in the way of explanation. For him it was an impossible situation. The possibility that the chief Watergate defendants might also be pardoned increased the angry reaction, and the next day the White House found it necessary to revise the statement.

This was done by Hushen's explanation that pardons for the Watergate defendants would be considered, if and when they applied through the normal channels, which would begin with applications filed through the Justice Department. At the time, no application had been filed. Hushen made it clear that Ford was not prepared to offer pardons to the defendants. But the error was never admitted for what it was. To have done so would have strengthened the credibility of the new administration, because the error was so glaringly apparent. Instead, the Ford White House chose to adopt orthodox White House methods. Hushen and others sought to explain the error away as a matter of semantics or misinterpretation, a favored device of the Nixon regime. It was clear to me that the new administration had accepted one of the myths of the Presidency: in that office *petty politics and gross human error do not exist* and thus cannot be admitted. The experience was a shattering one for Hushen, whose credibility had survived an assortment of Attorneys General, dating back to John N. Mitchell, but who, to his credit, obviously was not prepared for the insuperable politics of the White House. This incident could have been dismissed as a first stumbling effort of people new to the institution had it not been for what came later.

As successor to ter Horst, Ford picked Ronald H. Nessen, a reporter for the National Broadcasting Company who had been one of the small group of journalists assigned to cover Ford during his Vice Presidency and had moved to the White House when he became President. I had known Nessen only casually, but respected him as a reporter. I thought he, like Ford, would take a more conventional view of the White House and the role of the press secretary than ter Horst had taken, and for that reason I found it a little disturbing when he told reporters, "I will never knowingly lie to you, never knowingly mislead the White House press corps." If Ford was going to have a traditional administration, Nessen would find it hard to live with such a statement. Perhaps he could uphold the pledge not to lie outright. But misleading reporters was so much a part of the Washington scene, especially at the White House, that I did not see how any public relations officer could refrain for long from doing so. I thought Ford would have done better under the circumstances to have picked one of the few public relations veterans in the federal government who had managed to maintain the respect of both the officials they served and the press. None of them would have made such a statement, because they know there are times they are required to mislead the press. There are certain aspects of decision-making that officials invariably want kept secret, at times for legitimate reasons. For example, for a President to disclose a serious split within his administration on a policy issue would invite opposition in Congress and elsewhere. Thus his public relations apparatus must obscure the truth, or so it is believed in the executive offices of Washington.

In any event, Nessen was soon enmeshed in angry disputes with reporters, which I considered entirely normal for a conventional Presidency. The disputes were more intense because of the experience of Watergate and the fact that Washington journalists had become more bold and demanding. Nessen contributed his troubles largely to the raucous spirit of discord left over from the Nixon administration, but I thought his apparent acceptance of past practices in the office prevented his overcoming what certainly would have been a most difficult situation for anyone.

The most embittered dispute with the press at this writing occurred shortly after I left the White House beat, in the late spring of 1975. The commission, headed by Vice President Rockefeller, to investigate the past conduct of the Central Intelligence Agency had planned to release, as part of its report, a section dealing with the agency's role in assasination plots involving some foreign leaders, and sources on the commission so advised members of the press. Later, however, the President or some of his advisers thought it would be wise for the commission to refrain from comment on this sensitive subject. Here, one of the long-standing myths of the Presidency came into play: *There can never by any disagreement between the President and the Vice President.* During my years in Washington, I never heard the White House admit to even the slightest disagreement of any kind between the two officials or among their staffs. The Vice President or his staff would so admit, but never the President or his staff. Disagreement, in the White House view, smacks of disloyalty or disaffection on the part of the Vice President, whose will must always be bent to that of the President. Nessen could not bring himself to say that the President and his staff were in disagreement with the Vice President and his staff and simply overruled them. The press room was thrown into another turmoil and Nessen talked of resigning his job.

In the intervening months, there wore other examples that attracted less attention. The Ford White House showed no inclination to overcome the long-standing myth that *there is always substantial progress to be demonstrated in an area where the President has pledged progress or where he has a constituency he feels must be served.* In the area of benefits for war veterans, this myth had been maintained by a succession of Presidents, who proclaimed progress for veterans even while none was being made. Ford upheld the tradition in a Veterans' Day speech on October 29 in Arlington, Virginia. He said a special task force on employment for veterans had submitted a plan "for recruiting and hiring into the government at least 70,000 Vietnam veterans during fiscal year 1975. I am ordering the federal departments and the agencies to move and move now on this action plan to make sure these vets are hired as quickly as possible." A check of the records showed the jobs were not new ones at all. They had been in the budget for some time. Someone in the Presidential bureaucracy had come up with the jobs plan to make it appear the President was doing something for veterans, even though he was preparing to veto, for economic reasons, a bill that would have increased educational benefits by 23 percent.

The new press office was more relaxed than Nixon's had been about the myth that *the President always works hard, even when he is on vacation,* but maintained it nevertheless. During the Christmas season, when Ford was in Vail, Colorado, Nessen, in his briefings, always stressed the work that Ford was accomplishing, even though he seemed to be on the ski slopes or at dinner parties most of the time. Work was being accomplished, all right, as shown by the outpouring of messages, orders, and so on, but it was largely staff work. I thought it was a healthy thing that the President would take time off and delegate duties to others. Invariably, however, there always was criticism that the President was out frittering away his time while the country mired deeper into trouble, a result of the public myth about the Presidency, that *the man in office can somehow save the country by hard thought and work.* It is because of public expectations that the President's court feels obligated to maintain the work myth. Many people believe that Presidents are overburdened to the point of great suffering. I never saw any evidence to confirm that they were burdened by work. There is no doubt they carry a burden of responsibility, but much of their day-to-day duties is done for them. Before every meeting with a foreign or domestic visitor, a President is provided with a briefing paper on whatever subject they might discuss; before every interview and press conference he is handed a book representing many hours of staff work that will, within a few minutes, bring him up to date on every important issue; while traveling he can sleep on his bed aboard the Presidential plane, while others in the party are awake and working; at home and at travel, every conceivable step is taken to provide for his comfort and convenience.

Some of the Presidential myths are harmless in themselves, but frequently they get in the way of reporting the news. As a result, they perpetuate the aura of distrust between the Presidential staff and the press. The press secretary becomes the focal point of the discontent. During the morning gripe sessions in the press room prior to the briefings, which continued to be late and irregular, some of the reporters complained that Nessen was no better than Ziegler. I thought Nessen's sincerity in trying to do a competent job and the fact that he had a basic understanding of the public trust made such a comparison untenable. At the same time, the change in the press office from the Nixon period was not as great as I had thought it would be. Extraordinary skepticism on the part of the reporter was still a requirement and a reporter's perception frequently was a more reliable guide than official pronouncements.

The manner in which the White House operates is dependent to a large degree on the person in charge of the staff. Donald Rumsfeld, who quietly succeeded Haig as chief of staff a few weeks after Ford became President, brought a vast improvement for the public interest, I thought. He had been a bright young Republican congressman from suburban Chicago before Nixon, early in his first term, brought him into the executive branch where he held several jobs, the latter as ambassador to the North Atlantic Treaty Organization. He had served in the White House under Haldeman and thus knew first hand of the excesses during that period. Rumsfeld was generous with his time; I never had any trouble reaching or interviewing him if I really needed access and could get through the banks of secretaries who constantly stand between officials and reporters.

What bothered me about Rumsfeld was that he had been a part of the Nixon administration for so long and seemed typical of the smooth, buttoned-down young men of that period who got ahead quickly in government. After he had been in the Ford White House a short while, I wrote a story, based on statements of several persons close to Ford in and out of the White House, that between the November elections and the first of the year Ford would make some substantial changes in the cabinet he had inherited from Nixon. A few days later,

Rumsfeld was asked about the report in an interview on one of the television networks. He, in effect, denied any such plans. The *Times* dutifully carried his denial in full, even though it contradicted what I had written on good authority. The changes, in fact, did not take place as soon as my sources had indicated. But shortly after the first of the year, Ford made several new cabinet appointments while keeping several who had been appointed by Nixon, as planned in the early days of the Ford Presidency and as my story in November had forecast. I could understand Rumsfeld's reasoning. A President cannot signal the dismissal of a cabinet member in the newspapers and expect that official to satisfactorily carry out his job in the meantime. But the incident pointed out once again, the difficulty a White House reporter has in writing the truth if he depends on, or even takes into account, the public statements of officials.

As to reforming the institution, I concluded that Rumsfeld was tinkering, rather than attempting an overhaul. A great amount of authority was decentralized, from the White House back to the departments and agencies. But this was no more than a return to a system that had existed before Nixon put his radical plan for centralization into effect. As for the Presidential staff, Rumsfeld told me in an interview that the President was taking such action as reducing limousine privileges, which had been valued as a badge of prestige more than a method of transportation. He said the President was also reducing the size of the staff. The official budget that came out in January indicated there would be a 10 percent cut, and Ford said the same in a news conference on February 4. A check of the figures, however, showed that most of the reduction was in the legal staff Nixon had brought aboard to defend him against the Watergate charges. The staff would continue at about five hundred. I could never understand what all those people did to justify their substantial salaries. The President has the Office of Management and Budget, an elite agency numbering almost seven hundred employees, to advise him on every aspect of policy and government, and he has other Presidential agencies with personnel totaling about five hundred for specialized advice.

The Presidential staff has swollen over the years, I became convinced, largely to expand the White House public relations effort. At least one hundred of the five hundred staffers were directly involved in some type of public relations activity, and many of the others were engaged in some way in improving the President's public image. Even under the Kennedy administration, which had a special knack for manipulating the media, the press office had only a handful of people. Nessen had about forty-five, with a large stable of deputies and assistants at the top level. This in itself did not seem inflated, considering the large amount of work involved. Yet Ford kept the Office of Communications, which the Nixon administration had created as a blatant propaganda instrument. Ford retained the office as a means of going directly to the media and other agencies outside Washington to favorably advertise the President's policy and performance. He had a staff of five photographers and a contingent of Army Signal Corps photographers recording on film almost every movement of the President and his court. Ford expanded the White House Office of Public Liaison, which was one more effort to sell the President and his programs to highly placed persons across the country. Under William J. Baroody, Jr., the office would set up meetings with governors, mayors, business and labor leaders in the various regions. The meetings were advertised as an opportunity for an exchange of views on such subjects as the administration's economic and energy policy; but the White House, with the entire executive branch at its command, would order federal officials to turn out for the meetings in large numbers, making them, most of all, a substantial public relations effort for the administration.

What surprised me most about the Ford public relations apparatus was that within a few weeks he had as large, and even more structured, speech-writing staff than had served Nixon. There were about forty employees in the White House editorial office, including six full-time speech writers, all reporting to

Robert T. Hartmann, a Presidential counselor. One, Robert Orben, specialized in humor and was recruited from show business. The writers struggled to make the Presidential prose appear as pedestrian and folksy as Ford usually talked. I once saw a list of officials who had to review major Presidential speeches before they could be declared ready for the President's approval and delivery. There were more than twenty names on it. If a camel is a horse put together by a committee, then perhaps the production-line method of Presidential speechwriting explained why I never again heard a Ford speech that conveyed the simple eloquence of those delivered when he first took office.

Presidents, always embattled by the press, feel they need all the help they can get to obtain a fair hearing before the public. My feeling throughout the Nixon reign and my experience during the Ford period was that the cards were stacked against the press. Of the reporters who cover the White House regularly, those who have a close-up familiarity with what goes on there, only a handful are permitted by their organizations to write tough, critical pieces about what they see and hear. The vast majority of copy flowing out of the White House is an objective rendering of official statements and actions in the wire service mold. Beyond that, it does not seem right for democratic government to maintain, at public expense, a vast public relations apparatus for selling and reselling a public official. A President, with his broad powers and direct access to the public, can prevail without it and perhaps be a better President.

Aside from the public relations aspect, a large Presidential staff increases the opportunity for intrigue and infighting that invariably takes place around centers of power. Ford had not been in office more than a few weeks when signs of conflict and jealousy began to show. Ford himself did not seem to require the unquestioned loyalty of his subordinates that had been a mark of the Nixon administration. But some of his aides did not take so generous a view. For example, when Secretary of the Treasury William E. Simon expressed opinions on policy that differed from the official Ford position, some of the Ford aides began telling reporters that Simon would soon resign, but in the usual practice did not authorize use of their names. These reports became so numerous that Ford finally called Simon in, assured him he wanted him to stay and issued a statement that he was wanted in the administration. John C. Sawhill, director of the Federal Energy Administration, was not so fortunate. His outspoken, independent stance on energy policy created so much dissension within the White House staff that he was discharged.

The practice of White House aides anonymously leaking information about another member of the administration creates a special problem for the reporter. When an aide who is close to the President says that a certain official is leaving or is no longer in the good graces of the President, it is hard not to write it. In 1973, I wrote on good authority that Herbert G. Klein, a long-time Nixon associate, was leaving his post as director of the Office of Communications. Klein did leave within a few months. But I was sorry I had written the story when I learned that I was being used to ease Klein out. A reporter never knows the real motive of his source in leaking such information, because he does not have access to what is going on behind the scenes. The official involved must deny the report unless he is, in fact, on the verge of leaving. Confusion results and nothing is gained from that kind of reporting. After a few months on the White House I refrained as well as I was able from writing such stories, but it was not easy when I would be asked by an editor who could not know of the intrigue involved, about a report appearing as authoritative in another publication.

A large, structured staff in which scores of people are struggling for a share of authority makes intrigue inevitable. On a small staff of the kind maintained through the Roosevelt administration, there are fewer people seeking favored positions; there is no need for a tyrant, such as Haldeman, to keep them in place; and the spreading of derogatory reports about other administration officials is reduced because the source of the report is more easily traced. Even though the big increases in White House staff began under Truman and Eisenhower, an indication of how far things have gone since can be seen through Phillip E. Areeda, a Harvard Law School professor who served in the White House during the Eisenhower and Ford administrations. Areeda brought to the Ford White House a rare intellectual capability. Those who had known him in the past predicted that he would soon become a power in the new administration. His title was Counsel to the President, meaning he was one of the White House lawyers, but as such his assignments could have been unlimited. After a few months, however, Areeda resigned and returned to Harvard. Under Eisenhower, he said, he had been a very junior member of the staff, but even so, he felt he accomplished more then than he did as a senior member of the Ford staff, at least in part, because the Eisenhower staff was smaller and less structured. In the intervening time, the White House operation evolved into a complicated system of meetings, lines of authority, and formalities, to such an extent that even a person of considerable drive and intellectual power could have trouble breaking through with new innovations. But it was a staff most likely to continue the orthodoxy and the myths of the office.

When Ford became President, there seemed to be a public demand for a diminishing of the trappings of the office that tended to turn the heads of those who came to it. Ford did not have lavish vacation homes built for him, but he retained almost everything else within the law that had attracted criticism under Nixon. He traveled extensively—24,000 miles by the time he had been in office two and a half months—with the full use of jets, helicopters, limousines, advance men and security agents. He vacationed in lavish resorts—Vail at Christmas, Palm Springs at Easter—and hobnobbed largely with very rich industrialists who had attached themselves to Ford when he was minority leader. Ford was a plain man who could have helped ease the public distrust in government officials and gained polit-

ical points for himself by dispensing with all of this. The fact that
he did not, reinforced my conclusion that he held a most conventional view of the Presidency, unchanged by the lessons of
Watergate.

The bureaucracy did its share to continue the mystique of
the imperial Presidency. I was struck by this on November 1,
1974, when I was standing outside the Benson Hotel in Portland,
Oregon, where a crowd of demonstrators and admirers were
waiting for Ford to appear. He was then campaigning for
Republican congressman. His appearance was signaled by a
wave of stern Secret Service agents who cleared a path, shoving
aside those who did not move readily. One disheveled demon-
strator who tried to break through the line was thrown to the
ground. The President emerged smiling, and stepped into his
limousine. Agents swarmed onto his car and the following cars,
hanging from them in all directions as the entire motorcade
careened around the corners under full siren, like teen-agers
screeching off in sports cars. Every Presidential movement is
accompanied by the most urgent haste and attention on the
part of all concerned, as if the President were being rushed to
conduct some world-shaking business. In Portland, he was being rushed to and from one dull and inconsequential speech
after the other.

In use of its authority, the Presidency that Gerald Ford put
together was, overall, restrained and cautious. But it left intact
and strengthened all of the forms and structures that had contributed to the abuse of power in recent years. They were
preserved for the next elected President who would consider
himself to have a mandate, as virtually all Presidents do. That
was why it remained important to report what the institution
was as well as what it *did*.

15
THE LONGEST DAY

Almost every aspect of covering the Ford White House was easier, though duller, than it had been when Nixon was President. One exception was travel. Nixon wandered in search of a new vacation spot or a new office, or to save his Presidency. But once he arrived at a place and made the required public appearance he would go into seclusion and his entourage for the next few days became static. Ford, on the other hand, was gregarious and liked movement. Once he arrived at his destination he would not sit still. He was somehow attracted by the longest, most tiring dinners and receptions he could find in far-away places. The jostling and admiring crowds that greet every President stimulated him to more movement. The press, which felt obligated to trail him constantly but was much more encumbered in movement than the President, was frequently like the last little guy on the end of a crack-the-whip game.

To adequately report the White House it is necessary to make a good portion of the Presidential trips because the President takes with him not only most of the press office but most of his senior staff. The White House may be in Washington one day, the next in Melvin, Illinois, or any place the President or his staff might find alluring. One day—Monday, October 21, 1974—remains in my memory as the perfect illustration of what it is like to report the traveling White House.

I was assigned to the Air Force One pool (the new administration had not reached the point of using the pools for reward
or punishment) for Ford's trip to Mexico, his first venture outside the United States as President. It was necessary for me to
arise at 5 A.M. in order to arrive at Andrews Air Force Base for
a 7 A.M. departure. The press plane, which carried the luggage,
left even earlier. To get my bags on the press plane, I would
have had to arise at 4 A.M. I chose to sleep the extra hour, and
I arrived aboard the President's plane with a suit case, a porta-
ble typewriter, and a tape recorder, never anticipating what
was to come. The writing pool that day included Frank Cormier
of AP, Helen Thomas of UPI, and John Mashek of *U.S. News and
World Report*. On a Presidential jet no item for comfort and
luxury is overlooked. The seats are deep and cushy. In a few
moments we were all dozing. It had been a short weekend.
Ford was then in the midst of his exhaustive campaign for
Republican congressmen. He had stayed late Saturday night at
a fund-raising dinner in Louisville, and the press plane had
arrived back at Andrews long after midnight.

I had barely dozed off when someone punched me awake.
We were confronted by the formidable presence of Henry Kissinger, pink-cheeked, alert, grinning, and making jokes of our
lassitude. He was still very much the college professor instruct-
ing the uninitiated as he sketched the issues that would be
discussed by Ford and Mexican President Luis Echeverría Ál-
varez. They were important issues, but Kissinger said he was
making the trip mostly because of his friendship with Mexican
officials, that the journey was scheduled largely for Ford and
Echeverría to become acquainted. "The President could handle this with his left hand," Kissinger said. Helen Thomas was
alert enough to remind Kissinger that Ford was left handed. "I
mean with his right hand," Kissinger said, and everyone
laughed as reporters always do at a Kissinger briefing.

Writing the pool report fell to Mashek and me, because the
wire service reporters had to prepare their own copy for filing
immediately on arrival at Tucson, Arizona. Pool reports, to be

useful to all who use them, must be detailed. The task of condensing the Kissinger briefing and giving the background of the several issues involved took most of the flight time. At Tucson we boarded helicopters for the trip to the border town of Nogales, where the two Presidents were to meet, but which had no landing strip large enough to accommodate a 707 jet. I had to carry all of my luggage because I would no longer be a member of the Air Force One pool when the President flew out of Tucson late that night. Because of a shortage of helicopters, most of the White House press had been bused earlier to Magdalena, a farm town nestled in mountains sixty miles south of Nogales, where the main events of the day were to take place. Mashek and I thus had to write a full report on the events at Nogales.

In Nogales, the streets on both sides of the border were lined with children and adults carrying colored pictures of both Presidents and waving Mexican and American flags. Ford rode in an open-top car and waved to the crowds, who responded with cheers. At the center of the town, Echeverría greeted Ford and Kissinger with an *abrazo*, the traditional Mexican embrace, and the officials, in the midst of a great throng, moved onto a red-carpeted platform set up in the middle of the street for the ceremony. It was the largest and friendliest crowd Ford had seen since becoming President. The color of it was the kind of news that pre-empts much space and time in newspapers and newscasts.

It was hard to believe that so many enthusiastic people could be packed into so small a place. With my suitcase, typewriter, and tape recorder between me and the agitated Mexicans, I could not free my arms to take notes. In the confusion, members of the pool had separated. The schedule called for us to board a bus after the ceremony, but I could not find one that would take the pool. Ford and Echeverría decided to take an unscheduled stroll through the crowds, but the crowds only swept along with them. I was pushed for blocks before I finally found the press bus edging its way through the people. Mashek and others from the pool one by one found the bus and climbed aboard, perspiring and exhausted. The procession somehow moved to the helicopters and we were on our way to Magdalena. I do not remember what kind of helicopter carried the President, presumably one of the sleek new ones that the Air Force maintained for the White House. Ours was airy and noisy, so much so that ear stoppers, dispensed by members of the crew, were essential to preserve hearing. As we sat crowded together on bucket seats, shaken by the clattering engine, Mashek volunteered to attempt the typing on his knees as we composed the pool report of the tumultuous events in Nogales. He succeeded in producing a rough copy just as we set down on a field on the edge of the town. The props were still whirring as we disembarked, whipping dry sand and straw into our faces. I had forgotten to button my suit coat, which caught the wind like a sail and I thought for a moment I was going to take off, arms akimbo, clutching my suitcase in one and typewriter and tape recorder in the other.

Echeverría and Ford seemed bent on rubbing shoulders with the entire population of northern Mexico. They walked into the town and through the crowds gathered along the main street. Once again we were pressed from all sides by a mass of moving humanity that moved us slowly into the heart of town, where ceremonies were scheduled. By that time I was free of the pool obligation, had no need to cover all of the ritual and wanted to find a telephone to advise the *Times'* foreign desk what the story was likely to be. Norman Kempster of the *Washington Star-News*, asking directions in Spanish, found a passable route to the city hall, where a make-shift press room had been set up. We were only there a short time. Ford and Echeverría held a perfunctory private meeting after the ceremonies and left for Tubac, Arizona, for another meeting. By this time, several questions about the issues being discussed by the two Presidents had arisen, but no one I could find on the White House staff could supply the answers in the midst of the confusion. I had time left only to file a summary of my story before we were herded onto buses, which took us back to the helicopters.

It was now late afternoon in New York with the first edition deadline for the *Times* not far away. I tried to write my story on the vibrating helicopter, but I only succeeded in jamming the keys. There is no misery like that of a reporter with a spot story he cannot turn in in time for an edition. Knowledge that the world might be none the worse without the story does not relieve the discomfort. When the helicopter arrived at the Tubac Country Club, which some of Ford's Republican friends had made available for the occasion, my deadline was less than an hour away. A press room had been set up under a tent on the spacious lawn. I dashed off 1,000 words on the events of the day, barely in time for the edition. I had not eaten since breakfast. By the time I finished my story the buffet counter that had been set up in the tent was closed. I stole a roll from an abandoned plate.

Before the final meeting between the two Presidents ended, it began to rain, a phenomenon, I was told, that never happened in that region in October. There was to be a joint press conference by Ford and Echeverría in one of the larger rooms of the club. When we arrived in a herd to enter the building we were stopped and left standing for thirty minutes, in the rain. Both the U.S. and Mexican press had to be accommodated and the officials involved had to work out some orderly arrangement for the television crews, the reporters, and the cameramen. Once admitted, I could see neither President, seated at one end of the room, because of two rows of large posts holding up the ceiling and too many people and cameras. Worse, I could not hear half of what was being said. My second edition deadline was approaching—11 P.M. in New York. When it was over we bolted for the press tent to find the tables and telephones were being disassembled (no one had anticipated the events running so late and no one had thought to tell the workmen). It was now dark and there were no lights in the tent. We screamed in unison at the table wreckers. Several of us huddled around one that had been left and were barely able to see our notes by the headlights of cars parked outside. I could not see at all what I was typing, but wrote a lead anyway, saying that Echeverría had confirmed for Ford the discovery of substantial amounts of oil in southeast Mexico and that it would be put on the world market when developed. I left the copy with the Western Union telex operators, who were closer to the headlights, with instructions to make it out as best they could. I could not find a telephone that had not been disconnected to warn the foreign desk that the copy might be garbled. Never before had I written a story in the dark. The last press bus was about to leave. I stumbled aboard with my gear and found my reward for the day, a frosty bottle of Coors beer.

As the bus moved slowly through the rain, carrying us back to Tucson, I tried to analyze for myself how the working conditions of that day might affect White House reporting. For such conditions were not atypical. The day had been unusual only in that it had lasted longer than most. The *Times*, rightly I thought, had long had a rule that the difficulty a reporter might have in obtaining the story had no place in the copy. This was irrelevant and a burden to the reader. If journalism had an impact on government—the disputes between the President and the press, for example—that could be reported separately, and frequently was. Yet there could be no doubt that the news of a President's travels was shaped by the manner and extent of his movements, and such shaping was largely in the control of the White House. The press, except for whatever concessions it could extract by screaming at the press secretary, had to accept the arrangements made by the President's staff.

Travel in itself was no hindrance to reporting. I had always been stimulated by the sight of new places and the crowds that turned out to see a President, as were most reporters. Viewing the country dispels some of the parochialism and in-group attitudes that fester in Washington. If reflective, in-depth reporting was needed to adequately portray the Presidency, however, traveling in the White House manner hardly enhanced it. It was easy to become neurotic, as some White House reporters had long since been. The constant strain created a strange preoccupation for comfort and luxury. The White House Transportation Office usually booked us into the best hotels, but they were seldom fine enough. I never knew how Robert Manning and Ray Zook, the chief transportation officers, remained so cool and courteous in the face of all the grumbling and growling. Even in the worst days of the Nixon administration, the Transportation Office remained the one center of civility.

The frustrations, constant movement, and irregular hours led to more drinking than I thought was conducive to the best of journalism. My own consumption of alcohol had increased sharply since I joined the White House beat, I reminded myself as I reached for another Coors. To some, there seemed no other way to endure those long plane rides in the middle of the night. There was too much noise to either sleep or read and there had to be some way to uncoil from the labors of the day. John Mashek and I had a joke about the way the airline stewardesses would shove trays of Bloody Marys at us no matter how early we boarded. Once at Palm Springs, we stumbled aboard at 6 A.M. and sure enough, there were smiling stewardesses holding out not only Bloody Marys but screwdrivers. Everyone expected the White House press to be hard drinkers. Ford made a crack about it at the 1975 White House Correspondents Association dinner. At home the White House reporters and photographers probably consumed no more alcohol than others in the press and politics. On the road, alcohol was largely a pain killer. I never saw anyone too inebriated to do his job. There were teetotalers in the group, and some who abided by a rule of abstaining until the day's work was done.

When we reached the air base at Tucson, the President's plane had left two hours earlier, taking him to Oklahoma City, where he would resume his campaigning the next day. We found the gate to the airstrip closed. Two deadlines had passed since I left Tubac and I was not sure I had turned in satisfactory copy. There was no telephone in sight. After a half-hour wait, someone came and opened the gate. On the press plane there was a pool report saying Ford, in the rain and without a hat, had "worked the fence" before departure—in other words, shook the hands of admirers, probably the families of Air Force employees, who had turned out to see him. In Oklahoma City, there was another pool report on the reception Ford received as he drove into the city in the middle of the night.

I called the *Times* from my hotel room. The late editor seemed somewhat surprised when I inquired anxiously about my copy. The story was displayed prominently at the top of page one. "Was there some problem?" he asked. I told him it was written in the dark and I could not find a telephone and let it go at that. It was long after midnight. I looked at the schedule for the next day, Tuesday, October 22, 1974. The first event was at 7 A.M.

16
NEED FOR
A FRESH EYE

Once the Ford administration was in place, the overall press coverage reverted too quickly, I thought, to many of the old, pre-Watergate ways. The dark suspicions of officialdom on the part of the press that had deepened throughout the Nixon administration continued to such an extent that Nessen despaired of it, but this did not prevent the White House from once again taking charge of the story. In this, I thought, there was too much acquiescence, from the media.

Ford experimented with the press conference, holding it in different places within the White House and in different cities as he traveled the country. He permitted reporters a follow-up question in the event he did not answer the first one. This was a distinct improvement over past practice, because all public officials have a tendency to avoid the hard question. Some of us invariably abused the privilege, becoming so wrapped up in our own appearance at the center of the stage that we would ask the follow-up question whether it was needed or not.

The conferences were held frequently enough so that the most urgent questions were asked and answered in some fashion. Yet many of them seemed empty of substance. I attributed this not so much to Ford's dullness, as to the fact that his answers frequently came off the bureaucracy's production line, the product of the many hours of work that go into preparing a

President for a news conference. Also, many of the questions were too soft, too empty, or so long and redundant that they took valuable time from the answers. What came through in all of the press conferences and in his other television appearances, however, was the one quality the White House tried most to sell—that Ford was a nice guy. His speech writers, his television advisers, his press agents, all worked diligently to make sure this quality was apparent on television. It has been a custom for the senior wire service correspondent to end a conference with the words, "Thank you, Mr. President." It was and remains an appropriate formality to show respect for the office. But it is no more than a formality because it is the President who is largely being served. The press does not even determine when the conference will be ended. That is decided ahead of time, largely by the press secretary, to fit the needs of the show business requirements that the modern White House has adopted.

Ford reinstituted an old practice that Presidents had long used to advance a political position or some Presidential cause —the exclusive interview. Such interviews can serve the press and the public if they come at the right time and if handled with discretion by the interviewer. With Ford they became routine. From time to time he would make himself available to one of the newspapers, wire services, networks, or news magazines. In the exclusive interview, as in so many other formats at the White House, the President can command space and attention, whether or not he says anything that is news. Because an interview is exclusive and the President is the President, publications and broadcasters will give it space or time simply because nobody else has it. After the dearth of Presidential cooperation in the Nixon years, there was a scramble for the exclusive interview with Ford. Month after month they poured forth in great volume but were hardly ever worth the space or time given them. There was heavy emphasis on the photo essay or story of Ford at work, nearly always depicting him as the nice guy he is.

There was nothing wrong with this in itself. Ford as a nice guy was legitimate news. However, the critical aspect of the Ford Presidency during this period, a number of observers thought, was his questionable policies at a time of economic trouble at home and gathering crises abroad. Yet the focus of the White House press, with the help and direction of the press office, was largely on the Ford personality. Beyond that, the interview, like the press conference, is no place for a critical examination of policy and its application. Here the President puts across his point of view, and it was not unusual for him to advance the most bankrupt policy without the interviewer calling his hand on it. I thought a White House reporter's time was better served during this period in search for developments *he* thought important.

Almost anything the President did or said was considered news by much of the media, even while more significant developments were occurring unreported elsewhere. We were creatures of a generation of habit, conditioned by years of holding the office and the man too much in awe. Despite the lessons of the Nixon years, there was, I thought, an overabundance of undigested, uncritical rendering of the White House line in the media.

As a beat, the White House never lost its fascination for me, because of the difficulties it represented and the constant challenge of how I might get around them. For the critical reporter, it remained a mountain, largely unscaled. During my two years and four months on the beat, I had reconfirmed my belief that a reporter must be of independent mind, with his own conception of how a democratic institution ought to function, and shape his copy accordingly. It was no longer adequate, if it ever was, for a reporter to score beats and exclusives without questioning how the office operated, where it was going as an institution, and what were the motives of its occupants. The Washington press, in the past, I believed, had too readily acquired many of the barnacles and blind spots that inflicted the areas of government we were covering. For years, the media, with rare exceptions, had, out of habit, reported in considerable detail what Congress enacted in the way of legislation and policy without reporting also that it was a weakened, faltering institution overshadowed by the executive branch, which would twist legislation to its own will, and was unable to come to grips with many of the issues that were most important to the people.

Washington journalists, aside from the columnists and editorial writers, have been shackled in the past by their own self-restraint. They were always alert to reporting what government did but timid in questioning if government was functioning as it should. There is the reporter in Congress, for example, or in the Justice Department, or the State Department, who, in a bull session, gives a brilliant analysis of what is wrong with the institution, why and what is needed, yet his copy, over a period of years, would not reflect an inkling of this. In the complexities of modern government, someone has to make a judgment. I would trust the reporter, carefully making his point through documentation, over anyone in the institution or outside with a special interest to serve, or the columnist or editorial writer whose knowledge and contacts with the institution usually are more limited.

The danger for the Washington journalist is that he can easily be so influenced by the scene that he is covering that his judgment becomes blurred and he begins to think the way those he is covering do. In the spring of 1975, when I was addressing a group of foreign students who were studying American government, a perceptive young man from Indonesia, apparently sensing some ossification or stuffiness in Washington journalism, asked me if we did anything resembling the practice in some socialist countries of sending people back to small towns and lowly jobs occasionally for a renewal of spirit and perspective. My answer was certainly not, but that it might not be a bad idea. His point was particularly applicable for the White House beat. After a few months on the assignment, I formed the opinion that no reporter ought to stay there year after year. The pace was too intense for a prolonged criti-

cal performance. The tendency to become part of the court or
to become neurotic in resisting the blandishments of the office
was too great.

As the Ford administration settled in and as excitement
gave way to long periods of dullness, I found some of my attitudes changing. Rather than being offended by the press conference, as I had been in San Clemente, I began having such
thoughts as which of my suits would look best on television. I
began thinking about where Ford would spend the next holiday
and what kind of accomodations we would have, or how late the
press plane would get back from Nebraska.

In Palm Springs, Ford held a reception for the press at the
palacial home of a friend where he had spent the Easter holidays. He stood courteously and made small talk appropriate for
the occasion. But Kissinger soon drew most of the reporters
around him when he began talking foreign policy and saying
the United States needed in some way to demonstrate its intent
to uphold its commitments. Other members of the staff were
offended by Kissinger's apparent upstaging of the President
and said some harsh things about him. Ford, the next day at Las
Vegas, found it expedient to praise Kissinger lavishly in a
speech, apparently to quell any rumors of growing opposition
to him. The incident seemed too parochial for me to take much
interest. A fresh eye might be better for watching the President's court. I accepted an offer of another job on the *Times,* yet
I left reluctantly because the challenge was still there.

One day in the late spring, I went back to the White House
to clean my possessions out of the *Times'* desk. The press room
was deserted. Ford was out somewhere in the country making
a speech and all of the President watchers and his press agents
had gone with him. The teletype machines clattered away quietly in their boxes, bringing in the news for no one to read. I
wandered into the hall that led to the executive offices. The
guard's desk was empty and I examined for the last time the
colored pictures on the walls showing Ford, looking very Presidential, in various poses with various people. The Rose Garden,

still immaculately kept and visible through the sparkling glass, was vacant. The lawn seemed as if no foot had ever trod there. It was difficult to believe that this scene had been the center of so much tumult. I had to remind myself that down those corridors, somewhere, intrigue was still going on by staff members left behind. In the press room, one of the Ziegler stars that was suppose to signal something about coverage opportunities was flashing off and on, probably the result of a mispunched button. But I was glad that I still did not know the code.

INDEX